Debussy

Unlocking the Masters Series, No. 13

Series Editor: Robert Levine

Debussy

The Quiet Revolutionary

Victor Lederer

AMADEUS
PRESS

An Imprint of Hal Leonard Corporation
New York

Published in 2007 by Amadeus Press (an imprint of Hal Leonard Corporation)
19 West 21st Street, New York, NY 10010

Printed in the United States of America

Book design by Snow Creative Services

Library of Congress Cataloging-in-Publication Data is available upon request.
ISBN-10: 1-57467-153-7
ISBN-13: 978-1-57467-153-7

www.amadeuspress.com

For Bob Levine, my friend and *réalisateur*

Contents

Acknowledgments

Thanks again to Bernie Rose for shedding light on this very complex music; thanks as always to my children, Karen and Paul, and to my wife, Elaine, for their love and support.

Debussy

Listening to Debussy

Claude Debussy's stature as a major composer is generally accepted by audiences, and it is axiomatic among most professional musicians that he ranks with the very greatest. Yet his music often seems remote and difficult to grasp, with the result that much of his output is poorly understood.

It is clear when listening to Debussy that what one is hearing is beautiful, but its beauty turns out to be surprisingly hard to get one's ears around, and even harder to define. Some expect when starting to listen to Debussy that the music will be pretty and sweet, as they are drawn—misled, perhaps—by titles suggesting that there will be musical fairies, fauns, and water sprites; tinkly travelogues; and pastel-tinted nature scenes. The listener is then baffled by how strange and tough the music is, by how stubbornly Debussy refuses to gratify almost any preconceptions or knowledge of standard musical forms. The mature Debussy rarely begins pieces with a memorable, or even recognizable, tune; instead they fade in as if already in motion, and end by moving as though out of hearing. His harmonies are among the boldest—and strangest—ever conceived. With few significant exceptions—notably the symphonic poems *Ibéria* and *La mer*—his works lack the kind of big climaxes that excite audiences. His music also tends to be quiet: the thunderings of a Beethoven or a Brahms are not his style, and the dialectics of sonata form do not interest him. His music seems to meander gently, starting and often ending quietly. All seems to be in terms of elusive mood and color. Listeners need to retune their ears and minds to begin to grasp what Debussy is up to; only after a long period does one begin to understand that the eruptions of ecstasy are indeed there,

but they are arrived at by different means and often set at a lower—
or entirely different—pitch.

Few opera lovers would deny Debussy's *Pelléas et Mélisande* its spot
in the operatic pantheon, for example, but the work is among the most
difficult of all the great music dramas to appreciate. Here are no big
climaxes with the orchestra roaring as the singers belt out high notes;
instead, they seem to murmur their parts diffidently, just one note to
a syllable of text, supported by an orchestra that quietly underpins the
(entirely symbolic) action, breaking out violently only two or three
times. Indeed, *Pelléas* takes repeated hearings and viewings in an
opera house before the aptness of Debussy's treatment of his libretto
and the manifold, shimmering beauties of his score reveal themselves.
(Following this work with a score is highly recommended and easier
than it may sound.)

The chance that *Pelléas* will supplant *Rigoletto,* or even Wagner's
four-hour *Die Walküre,* in popularity is very slim indeed: it lacks the
thrust of Verdian drama or the glorious blaze of a Wagner score. And
yet, after even a couple of hearings, quiet moments reach out to snare
the sympathetic ear and heart as Pelléas entangles himself in the tendrils
of Mélisande's long, lovely hair.

The oratorio-like "mystery play" *Le martyre de St Sébastien,* though
very beautiful, has baffled listeners with its peculiar structure and
moments of utter strangeness since its 1911 premiere. It is never performed as originally conceived, but instead subjected to a variety of
reductions into manageable concert form and even further concentration into orchestral suites of highlights. In the small, exquisite world
of the French art song, Debussy's works are genuinely magnificent but
recondite and hard to grasp. According to some who have sung them,
they are exceedingly difficult to elucidate in performance.

Listeners are clearly far more comfortable with Debussy's instrumental works. Among the works for orchestra, the rich colors of the
Prélude à l'après-midi d'un faune (track 1 on the CD at the back of
the book) and *Ibéria,* with its brilliant instrumentation and fantastic
rhythmic snap, have found general popularity; the greatness of *La mer*
has always been overwhelmingly clear. The piano music is perhaps the
best-appreciated category of all, with pianists learning, performing,

and, when possible, recording the *Études* and both sets of *Préludes* as a rite of passage. In this category the cream has risen, with the early *Suite bergamasque* now yielding pride of place to the mature *Préludes* and *Images*. The tiny body of Debussy's chamber works, although revered by professionals, suffers from the neglect and misunderstanding of the class as a whole.

After listening to *Clair de lune* or *La fille aux cheveux de lin* (The Girl with the Flaxen Hair, track 9), the novice or casual listener drawn into further explorations of Debussy's music will often find surprising resistance. Sweet, easily digestible pieces like these turn out to be very much in the minority within the composer's output. Debussy's rhythmic agility presents no real obstacles, but his bold harmonic sense and wispy, fragmentary melodies can disorient and frustrate. Musical harmony consists in the way notes sounded at or nearly at the same time react with each other; and although Debussy composed music in the standard twenty-four keys (C major, A minor, and so on), he modified them so completely, employing dissonance so freely, that his music has a hazy, floating quality that makes it instantly recognizable as his.

Debussyan melody is unconventional, as well, often built from small components, and subjected to development only when doing so suits a structural purpose. When his tunes recur, they are rhythmically intensified or reclothed in strange harmonies as dreamlike recollections; triumphant thematic reincarnations are few but notable, as in *La mer*. Unlike themes by almost every composer before him, which are generally shaped to make themselves as articulated and memorable as possible, Debussy's are abstract and referential. Listen, for example, to the main theme of the piano work *L'isle joyeuse,* which, although obviously carefully sculpted, also sounds veiled and distant. There are countless other examples of ironic metamelodies throughout Debussy's oeuvre, and much of what he wrote, such as the Spanish-flavored works, are *recherché* music *about* music. Complex, sophisticated, modernist, Debussy's music takes work to get to know well: it is not for kids or the casual.

Debussy's genius was nourished by an unusually wide variety of musical streams. All were effectively and completely assimilated into Debussy's own style, with his mature works sounding wholly characteristic and original, never derivative. Influences include the third-tier composer Jules Massenet (1842–1912), famous today chiefly for his operas, especially *Manon* and *Werther*. From Massenet he seems to have learned his elegant compactness of forms and cool lyricism. Debussy's output generally is permeated with a very French reserve that makes emotional eruptions all the more potent.

Debussy was taken with the sound of medieval music, particularly the droning church music known as *organum*. Although the rules of classical composition forbade the extensive use of its archaic harmonic intervals, Debussy employed these regularly. Perhaps the most famous example of medieval influence is found in one of his best-known works for piano, *La cathédrale engloutie* (The Engulfed Cathedral), the strange and magnificent work that is the tenth of the first book of preludes.

Two great contemporaries of Bach, François Couperin (1668–1733) and Jean-Philippe Rameau (1683–1764), composed many suites for keyboard in which gravity and playfulness mingle beneath vivid musical surfaces. Many of these are "character pieces," descriptive music with titles that tell what or whom the piece describes. One of Rameau's most familiar character pieces is *La poule* (The Hen), in which the clucking of the bird is wittily imitated by the keyboard. This work, and many others by Rameau and the other *clavecinistes,* importantly prefigures the individual movements that make up Debussy's mature suites for piano, particularly the twenty-four preludes, each of which has a descriptive title. Debussy revered these masters proudly as his national musical ancestors; he played their works himself and modeled some of his own directly on their tightly wrought forms, most notably in the two grave sarabandes that are the second movement of the suite *Pour le piano* and *Hommage à Rameau* (track 7 on the CD) from the first set of *Images*. Debussy also conceived much of his keyboard music formally like theirs, in groups of short pieces of varied character.

It has been suggested with ponderous humor that all the greatest Spanish composers are from France. It is true that many French composers from the middle of the nineteenth century forward found themselves fascinated by the sharp rhythms, bright instrumental colors, and harsh melodic profile of Spanish popular song and dance. The list of great evocations of Spain by composers from north of the

Pyrénées is long and very distinguished. From Bizet's *Carmen,* which had its premiere in 1875, to the onetime pops favorite *España* (1883) by Emmanuel Chabrier, to the many Spanish-flavored masterpieces of Ravel and Debussy, French composers grasped the musical essence of their neighbor to the south with precision and brilliance. Debussy's Spanish works are many and varied in size and scope, from the massive orchestral eruptions of *Ibéria* to the smoky, nocturnal delicacy of *Soirée dans Grenade* (Evening in Granada; track 5), from the *Estampes* for piano, to the passionate but playful Cello Sonata (tracks 14 through 16). Debussy assimilated Spanish influences into his music with metabolic efficiency, to extraordinarily powerful results.

Another exotic musical influence was in the music of Java, which Debussy heard in 1889 at the *Exposition Universelle*—basically a world's fair—in Paris. This was a time when orientalism, fascination with all things from the Middle and Far East, was a major fad in the West. Javanese music, like that of a number of other Eastern musical systems, works from a different, far smaller, series of tones than the twelve notes of the mainstream Western scale, and it has a different, less event-driven structure, as well. And of course Javanese music is also based on the sound of instruments, particularly the *gamelan* orchestra, that had not been heard in late nineteenth-century Paris. Like many musicians who heard their Javanese counterparts perform, Debussy was overwhelmed by the beauty, delicacy, and sheer foreignness of the music from the Southeast Asian island; he never got over it, and its influence can be heard in many of his mature works for piano.

Among the Western composers admired and digested by Debussy were Bach and Mozart, but their influences are impossible to point out specifically. He claimed to dislike the conflict-driven music of Beethoven, whom he once referred to as *le vieux sourd*—"the old deaf one"—and purposely took his own in an entirely different direction (Nichols, *Debussy Remembered* 157). The brilliance of Franz Liszt's style can be heard echoed in much of his piano music, particularly the more virtuosic of the etudes and preludes. Liszt also had a profound effect on his style, with the wayward melodies, bold harmonies, and self-determining forms of some of the Hungarian master's late works sounding remarkably prescient of Debussy. It was Liszt who first made the piano depict water, which he did with immense success in a number of works, including *Les jeux d'eaux à la Villa d'Este* (The Fountains at the Villa d'Este), *Au bord d'une source* (On the Bank of a Spring), and the late masterpiece *La lugubre gondola* (The Mournful Gondola). Debussy's debt to Liszt for these discoveries is incalculable, as is that of his younger contemporary Maurice Ravel (1875–1937). Liszt's pianistic waters always ripple and flow, but depictions of water that moves in massive waves or that is nearly still are Debussy's own.

Debussy revered Mussorgsky, particularly his masterwork *Boris Godunov;* the darkness and daring of the tremendous music drama made a lasting impression. The titanic, dissonant block chords that imitate tolling of giant bells in the opera's Coronation Scene echo long and loudly through Debussy's work. Their harmonic boldness and vivid tone painting, the use of music to create a visual image in the mind of the listener, inspired Debussy, who admired the freedom of Mussorgsky's imagination and strove to impart the same openness to his own works.

The angular rhythms of early ragtime jazz resonated powerfully in the composer's mind, with his mature piano works including a number of well-known dances representing his (very French) adoration of American popular music. Most famous of all is *Golliwogg's Cakewalk* from the *Children's Corner,* followed by two marvelous preludes, *Minstrels* and *Général Lavine—excentric* from the first and second sets, respectively. It is a pity that Debussy did not live to hear the sea change in jazz initiated by Louis Armstrong in the 1920s, for he surely would have admired and drawn inspiration from that master's revolutionary syncopations.

The broadest and most profound influences on Debussy were the works of Chopin and Wagner, two of the nineteenth century's boldest musical imaginations. Admiration for Wagner peaked early in Debussy's career, waning sharply as he saw his own aesthetic at odds with that of the late-romantic titan.

Debussy made two pilgrimages to the Wagner theater in Bayreuth, Bavaria. On the first, in 1888, he saw *Die Meistersinger* and *Parsifal;* on the second, one year later, he saw *Tristan und Isolde.* The intensity of Wagner's music shattered the young Frenchman, as it did—

and does—legions of musicians and music lovers. And the sound of Wagner's radical chromatic harmony—slippery and seeming never to touch bottom—in act 3 of *Tristan* made an impression on Debussy that echoes distantly through much of his own oeuvre, as well. Wagner's harmonic thought—the floating, shockingly sensuous sound of unresolved dissonance that marks the breaking point of romantic and the border with modern—is the springboard from which Debussy launched his own equally daring experiments in harmony. On a different level he adopted, metabolized, and transformed Wagner's technique of thematic identification and development, the *leitmotiv.* This German word, meaning "leading motif," elliptically describes the pithy themes Wagner composed to identify and describe characters, objects, and situations in his operas. These he subjected to symphonic transformations over the course of each opera, or, in the case of the *Ring* cycle, four operas.

Wagnerian echoes are clearest in Debussy's early works, particularly the cantata *La damoiselle élue* of 1887 and 1888. Wagner's enormous influence on the young Frenchman, however, turned sour. Debussy later claimed to despise the German's work, but in this posture there were surely nationalistic pride and contrarianism, both strong traits in his character. By the time Debussy began to write *Pelléas* in 1893, he had digested Wagner and moved on, having found his own mature voice as a composer. His single operatic masterpiece does employ leading motifs to identify the main characters, but everything is much more muted and restrained than in Wagner. The floating, blurry harmony—the characteristic Debussy sound—is fully developed in *Pelléas et Mélisande,* which, like *Tristan und Isolde,* is one of the landmarks and turning points of Western music. But *Pelléas* sounds only like Debussy, and nothing like Wagner.

In his essay "The Naiveté of Verdi" (Weaver and Chusid, 1–12), the historian Isaiah Berlin expands on the German poet Friedrich Schiller's distinction between naïve and sentimental, using the former to describe artists whose work is unself-conscious, direct, and without irony. Working comfortably in existing forms, they tell their stories forcefully but plainly. (Verdi, accompanied by Homer, Shakespeare, Cervantes, Bach, and Handel, falls into this category.) For sentimental artists, the opposite is true: their works, marked by intentional complexity, torment of spirit, irony, and self-reference, display all the woes of the modern urban soul. Of course Wagner is one such, along with Dostoyevsky, Marx, Nietzsche, Baudelaire, and the other prophets of the split and tortured psyche. And so is Debussy, whose allusive music, filtered through an aesthetic of his own construction, is about how the composer hears his world, aural images, music that has come before, and pure sound itself. Debussy's music, like Wagner's, is sophisticated, profound, and profoundly beautiful—but neither simple nor direct.

"'Chopin is the greatest of all,' [Debussy] used to repeat. 'For with the piano alone he discovered everything'" (Marguerite Long, qtd. in Nichols, *Debussy Remembered* 178). Debussy had a deep love for and understanding of the music of Chopin, the poetic and heroic master of the piano, who broke every conceivable mold with his utterly individual style built of a grasp of keyboard sound perhaps equaled—but never surpassed— by only Liszt and Debussy. Apart from his brilliant melodic gift, Chopin commanded a harmonic vocabulary of unbelievable breadth and boldness, and a revolutionary formal inventiveness in which the content of a work determined its structure. Chopin's most daring works had to wait a century after his death to be widely appreciated, but Debussy knew the full measure of their greatness at once.

Unlike that of Wagner, the Polish composer's impact on Debussy was entirely salutary, considerable from the beginning and growing as the years passed. It was Chopin, rather than Wagner, whom Debussy came to view as his chief musical ancestor: "He was, as it were, impregnated by that composer's work, and through his own appreciation tried to convey all that he thought proceeded from the great Polish master," wrote pianist Marguerite Long (qtd. in Nichols, *Debussy Remembered* 175). The intense expressivity of the music within Chopin's forms, large-scale and small-, his harmonic terseness, and his ability to conceive in terms of the piano's tonal resources, anticipated and inspired Debussy's own formal and harmonic boldness and willingness to transform color and texture into primary musical elements.

It was from Chopin also that Debussy learned the dignity and value of short forms, notably the etude and prelude, into which the Polish master unstintingly poured his genius. The gigantism of Wagner's operas created a natural obstacle—a huge aesthetic mountain range—

for Debussy, like all composers who followed the German. Debussy, like many others, looked instead for creative inspiration to Chopin's deep mining of small forms on a solo instrument. Chopin's short forms contain worlds of emotion and bold musical ideas, as do Debussy's.

In 1914, at the suggestion of his publisher, Debussy undertook the editing of Chopin's works, the experience further deepening Debussy's reverence; in the following year he published his own etudes, dedicated to Chopin's memory. These and the preludes for piano are Debussy's most obvious tributes to two of the forms deepened so bravely by Chopin, but the earlier composer's fingerprint can be found in countless other places and ways. One of Debussy's favorite works by the Polish master was the *Barcarolle,* op. 60, which he played and taught often (Nichols, *Debussy Remembered* 55; Samson 257, 326n) and from which he learned much. It is not difficult to hear in this large-scale master-piece much that would become the trademark Debussyan sound, with a booming opening note in the bass, its sophisticated, protomodern harmonic scheme, and its intense and idiomatic use of the resources of the piano. It is in the sumptuous colors of the *Barcarolle*—an infinitely rich, hazy, glowing keyboard sound—that one can hear the clearest anticipation in Chopin of Debussy.

Most of Debussy's mature works carry descriptive titles to guide the listener to a clearer understanding of each piece's expressive content and purpose. One of Debussy's most important aesthetic goals was that his music evoke a visual response. The mysterious but undeniable abil-ity of sound to evoke a picture in the mind has long been recognized and has been a tool employed by almost every composer, including the most revered. The greatest names have employed pictorialism or tone painting, with Renaissance masters using rising melodic figures in their church music to describe a heavenward ascent.

A fugue from Bach's *Well-Tempered Clavier* or the opening movement of a piano sonata by Beethoven employs musical techniques that express emotion—joy, sorrow, or a sense of struggle are common—but these works do not generally evoke a picture in the mind of the listener. Nor, as abstract music, are they meant to. But when Beethoven imitates birdcalls or a thunderstorm in his *Pastorale* symphony, his goal, obvi-ously, is to make the listener "see" the birds and the rain. It is from roughly this position that Debussy composed, although in a way that makes Beethoven's musical pictures seem naïve in comparison. Once he reached his maturity in the 1890s, Debussy surpassed all composers in fusing the aural and visual, disarming the foolish prejudice against pictorialism. Debussy made this comment in a 1901 review of a concert: "In Bach's music it is not the character of the melody that affects us but rather the curve . . . the music will impress the public as regularly as clockwork, and it will fill their imagination with pictures" (Lesure 27). These words, revealing as to the fusion of sound and sight in Debussy's own mind, also go a long way toward explaining the elusive nature of his melodies. Unlike those by Mozart, Chopin, or Verdi, which are sculpted with strong profiles to make them memorable, Debussy's often emerge from the patterns of their accompaniments.

Debussy seems to have struggled mightily to find for every composition the precise sound and form that met his expressive goal. He dreaded the burden of developing an idea he considered banal or mediocre (Nichols, *Life* 159), screening his own mercilessly to work only with what could ultimately emerge seemingly weightless and effortless, like natural sounds. In a task that requires as much discipline as it does talent, Debussy further trained himself not to rush to write down his ideas, "so as to allow complete freedom to those mysterious inner workings of the mind which are too often stifled by impatience" (qtd. in Nichols, *Life* 32). His rewards were correspondingly immense: "The emotional satisfaction one gets from it can't be equaled, can it? . . . This power of the 'right chord in the right place'" (qtd. in Nichols, *Life* 156).

It is helpful, as well, to understand the heady artistic ferment of the extraordinary decades before and after the turn of the twentieth century. Wagner's shadow loomed quite terrifyingly over the musical world. Photography had challenged, then changed forever the nature of painting, forcing painters and sculptors to find new aesthetic goals and techniques to replace the hard lines of realism, supplanted by the new technology that had itself quickly become an art. The impressionism of Monet, Renoir, and Pissarro, the symbolism of Gauguin, and the postimpressionist experiments of Van Gogh and Cézanne were the resultant movements in France. There was also considerable interest in the art of the Far East, especially that of Japan.

The solipsistic, sometimes outrageous verbal forays of the poets Paul Verlaine and Charles Baudelaire stood at the vanguard of French literature before 1900, which would soon be dominated by the colossal outpouring of Proust's *À la recherche du temps perdu* (In Search of Lost Time, a title formerly mistranslated into English as *Remembrance of Things Past*) between 1913 and 1927. Debussy knew Baudelaire well, setting many of his poems as songs, as he did with a number of Verlaine's verses. Stephane Mallarmé's poem *L'après-midi d'un faune* (The Afternoon of a Faun) was the direct inspiration for one of Debussy's greatest, most famous, and groundbreaking orchestral works. The Belgian symbolist poet Maurice Maeterlinck's 1892 play *Pelléas et Mélisande* is another. This of course is the play that Debussy adapted very slightly to serve as the libretto for his single operatic masterwork.

Debussy craved visual stimulation compulsively, collecting Oriental knickknacks and objets d'art from an early age and filling his home with sketches and paintings. He was also an inveterate visitor to galleries and museums, loving—needing—to look at pictures. He expressed envy for his counterparts in the visual arts for being able to capture the essence of something in the natural world with a sketch of a few lines, an expressive luxury denied to composers, who cannot publish or hope to see performed works that are incomplete, unfinished.

The common categorization of Debussy as an impressionist in histories of music is on the mark but also misleading, and in any case not terribly useful from a musical standpoint. While his music provides countless powerful impressions of what it musically describes, the images it evokes are anything but blurry. As the biographer Edward Lockspeiser correctly observed, the word *impressionist* "is likely to convey none of the minute accuracy of expression, which, for both the interpreter and the listener, must after all be the paramount consideration" (156).

The "impressions" Debussy evokes are deeply rooted in perception and in the power with which the external world impregnates the senses. One may hear a sound or a name, catch a scent, or see a picture that seizes the mind and spirit, later to learn that this perception was incorrect in some factual way. Still struck by the intensity of the initial impression, one is unwilling to abandon its personal meaning, the sound, sight, or scent having become real as it was first perceived. Fog may be nothing but a ground-hugging cloud, but in the piano prelude *Brouillards* (Fog; track 10), Debussy captures the awe, edged with panic, that it summons. At the deepest level, Debussy's music describes the wonder of that initial perception and the adoration for it that fades only slowly, stubbornly, painfully. (The fading of the impression's initial power is, perhaps, a source of the melancholy that saturates his work.) His explorations of how the mind perceives, processes, and remembers stand as singular achievements not only in Western music, but in Western art.

Like the visual artists of his time, Debussy understood that an age was ending and that new means of expression had to be found. Like them, he had to move from the hard, clear lines in painting of form, in music of memorable melody, underpinned by predictable harmony, and thematic developments. Most important, and perhaps most comparable to his colleagues in the visual arts, was his raising of color—tone color—to primary importance. The mature Debussy's tonal palette, combined with his dislocated harmony, compares admirably with a haystack shimmering in the sun as painted by Monet: both redistribute the basic materials of their art into new textures, with new, revelatory expressions the result.

His Life

Debussy was famous before he was thirty, but there are significant gaps in the record until then—and after, as well. His life,
like that of many musicians, lacks the monumental events that
pepper the biographical pages of soldiers and politicians. Artists must
spend inordinate amounts of time in the act of creation, which requires
steely discipline of the sort few can imagine. Claude Debussy spent
much of the life for which he is remembered and revered sitting at a
piano, smoking cigarettes, playing a few notes, muttering and singing
to himself, before finally making a few jottings on his music paper. His
life might not unfairly be summarized: he was born, he worked in the
self-sacrificing manner of a great artist, and he died.

Debussy's character, to the limited extent it has come down to
us, was elusive. His nature, necessarily volcanic and passionate, was
repressed beneath layers of reserve, irony, and artistic discipline.
Eruptions of temperament appear to have been few. Like many whose
work is self-referential, however, he seems not to have been a "nice"
man: certainly his abandonment of his first wife, Lily, seems inexcus-
ably cruel. Yet he wielded an immense, playful charm and humor, and
was adored by his circle. Perhaps to balance the ugliness of his desertion
of Lily, his relationship with his daughter (whose name was Claude-
Emma but who is referred to only by his affectionate nickname for her,
"Chouchou") was marked by the deepest affection.

Debussy was born in the Parisian suburb of Saint-Germain-en-Laye
on August 22, 1862. His parents, both of modest background, had their
origins in Burgundy, the ancient east-central province that is home

to some of the country's noblest wines and is sometimes referred to as *la France profonde*—deep France. Manuel Debussy, the father, sold chinaware but was intellectually ambitious and music loving. He was also a radical, who was jailed for a year after the defeat of the socialist militant group known as the Communards. The composer's mother, born Victorine Manoury, was volatile and ill-equipped for child rearing. She sent at least two of her younger children away to be raised by their aunt, Manuel's sister (Nichols, *Life* 6). Claude enjoyed the dubious distinction of being the high-strung Victorine's favorite. How her character would have affected that of her son is easy to imagine; its effect on his genius cannot be gauged.

Debussy displayed an early aptitude for music that his parents wanted developed, with piano and general lessons from several second-string teachers following. Mathilde de Sivry, who called herself Madame Mauté de Fleurville, claimed to have studied with Chopin, apparently common enough among French piano teachers of the late nineteenth century. Although Madame Mauté de Fleurville seems not in fact to have been a pupil of the Polish master, she was an inspiring teacher anyway, and Debussy later wrote and spoke of her with the highest regard.

Debussy's character—dreamy, reserved, alternately grouchy and gracious—was apparently well set in his early years. His sister later wrote that he was "uncommunicative and closed in upon himself, liking neither his lessons nor his games. . . . He would spend whole days sitting on a chair and thinking, no one knew of what" (qtd. in Lockspeiser 6). His refined aesthetic sense also was evident from early on. He developed early a taste for fine food and objets d'art, cutting illustrations from books and mounting them on the walls of his room.

Debussy's musical gifts were obvious enough to secure his admission in 1873 to the Paris Conservatory, the great music school of France, more or less equivalent to the Juilliard School in the United States. Here he received rigorous training in musical theory that he would master, then shatter to bits. The posture of the conservatory was conservative, if not quite reactionary. Early on, Debussy studied the highly demanding training technique known as *solfège,* in which students sight-read, transpose to different keys—also at sight—and quickly analyze harmonic and contrapuntal textures. Yet of all the greatest composers, Debussy is surely the one whose music is least impregnated with counterpoint. He would later comment, "I don't write in the fugal style because I know it" (qtd. In Nichols, *Life* 58), as he strove to purify his own music from all outside influences, to pursue instead an intensely focused search for original ideas and sounds. Debussy had as much musical discipline as any composer, but in his maturity he learned to employ it in a contrarian way, deliberately breaking the rules.

Debussy was also developing into a great pianist, albeit one with an individual style and touch. He would later be known, as his idol Chopin had been, as a player of the greatest subtlety, with the ability to create an uncanny delicacy of tone and infinite shadings of volume. But Debussy won no awards at the conservatory for his playing, dashing any hopes that he might make a career as a virtuoso.

Already audacious in his harmonic thinking, Debussy inevitably outraged the more old-fashioned faculty at the conservatory with his experimental nature and blunt tongue. When one asked Debussy sarcastically what rules of harmony his unresolved dissonances followed, the young genius's reply *"Mon plaisir"*—"My pleasure"—would ring down the ages. But of course there were other faculty who showed understanding of and respect for Debussy's burning need to find expression for the sounds in his imagination. One also introduced him to the music of Wagner.

In 1880, in an interesting confluence of musical cultures, Debussy's piano teacher Antoine Marmontel helped to engage the young musician as a pianist in the entourage of Madame Nadezhda von Meck, the wealthy Russian widow who was Tchaikovsky's patroness. The tale of that tormented composer and the woman who adored and supported him, but refused ever to meet him face to face, is strange and fascinating. Debussy served as her household pianist for her travels in Russia and western Europe during the summers of 1880, 1881, and 1882. In a letter to Tchaikovsky in July 1880, von Meck wrote that Debussy's pianistic "technique is brilliant, but he lacks any personal expression." She later wrote that he could sight-read—that is, play music while reading it from the score without preparation—"splendidly" (Lockspeiser 12).

He and von Meck seem to have had a genuine affection for each other. A little dance by Debussy sent by von Meck to Tchaikovsky received a mixed review from the Russian; the two composers never met, although Debussy would later make it his business to meet as many other composers as he could.

Around this time, Debussy began an affair with Marie-Blanche Vasnier, a beautiful young woman married to a much older man. Many of Debussy's earliest songs date from this period; she is the dedicatee of most of those composed between 1880 and 1884. Eugène Vasnier, the husband of Debussy's lover, was nothing but kind to the composer, feeding him regularly, lending money that was never repaid, and offering encouragement when Debussy felt hopeless. It is in his relationships with the Vasniers that the selfish, unkind, opportunistic Debussy is first apparent. While an affair between a magnetic single artist and a married woman is both ordinary and not, with all its unknown variables, to be judged more than a century later, Debussy's multiple betrayals of his benefactor are surely unattractive. It is also the first manifestation of his inability to handle money, a trait he would never lose, though again, it was a common enough weakness.

In addition to the songs, Debussy began work on the first piece that brought him renown in the French musical establishment. This is the cantata *L'enfant prodigue* (The Prodigal Son), based on the biblical parable. The music, which shows an obvious reliance on Wagner's late style and is mild in comparison to that of Debussy's maturity, won for the young composer the conservatory's highest award, the 1884 Prix de Rome. Despite his defiance of rules and prickly personality, his stock had risen steadily among the conservatory faculty, as well as with his fellow students over the years, as his originality and technical facility could not be denied. Twenty-two members, including the eminent Charles Gounod (composer of *Faust*), of the twenty-eight-person committee voted for *L'enfant prodigue,* commenting that it offered "a very definite sense of poetry, brilliant, warm coloring, [and] lively, dramatic music" (qtd. in Nichols, *Life* 20). Debussy himself later professed sorrow at winning, sensing that he would never again be free; indeed, fame, with all its attendant miseries, found him at that moment.

Debussy was unhappy throughout two and a half years of the three he was supposed to spend in Rome, beginning in January of 1885. His task in Rome was to compose over the three-year program a large-scale work; he made several runs at writing an opera, none of which were finished, though he did begin the two-movement symphonic poem *Printemps* (Spring), his earliest orchestral work that is performed with any regularity.

Despite his constant griping, he had a number of incomparable musical experiences, absorbing and adoring the vocal music of the Renaissance masters Palestrina and Lassus, and attending a performance by Franz Liszt, the old lion of the piano. This was for Debussy "the greatest musical treat of his life" (qtd. in Lockspeiser 29). Debussy later played for the master, who apparently dozed off during his performance. In Milan, Debussy met Arrigo Boito, the brilliant librettist of Verdi's late masterworks *Otello* and *Falstaff,* and, with a letter of introduction from Boito, called on the great man himself. There is also the charming story of Debussy's meetings with Brahms in Vienna in 1887. After some initial bearishness by Brahms, the two apparently became friends. They discovered a shared love of Bizet's *Carmen,* a work hugely admired by many composers, and even attended a performance of it together; these two masters, whose approaches to composition are diametrically opposed, parted affectionately (Lockspeiser 43–46).

Feeling his way with some confidence as an artist, Debussy left Rome for Paris in the spring of 1887, half a year before the end of the Prix de Rome program. As a composer who now had the resources to bring his own talent to fruition, he no longer needed the conservatory. But 1887 begins a dark period in his recorded life. Apart from the few works he published, early in style but fairly distinguished nonetheless, little is known of his life. Music from this era includes the songs based on poems of Baudelaire, and the choral work *La damoiselle élue* (a setting of Dante Gabriel Rossetti's poem "The Blessed Damozel"), which represents a major advance from its predecessor, *L'enfant prodigue.* In these works, Debussy's voice is far clearer, as he strove successfully to purge all Wagnerian influence from his work.

During trips in 1888 and 1889 to Wagner's theater at Bayreuth, Debussy saw *Parsifal, Die Meistersinger,* and *Tristan und Isolde.* The effect of these towering works was profound, but Debussy was by then looking for his own way. If Wagner provided a negative stimulus, the Javanese music and dance Debussy watched and listened to at the Exposition Universelle of 1889 blew his conceptual doors and windows wide open. It was at this time, too, that he began to hear music of the great Russian nationalist composers, including Balakirev, Rimsky-Korsakov, and, above all, Mussorgsky, whose disdain for traditional Western forms and methods would further embolden Debussy.

All these influences came to a head in the watershed years of 1892 and 1893. It was then that Debussy found his true voice, composing his first masterpieces, the String Quartet in G minor, and the orchestral poem *Prélude à l'après-midi d'un faune.* He also read *Pelléas et Mélisande* by the Belgian symbolist playwright Maurice Maeterlinck, to which he felt an immediate attraction, and for which he began to sketch music. In 1893 he visited Maeterlinck at his home in Ghent, securing his permission to create a libretto from the play and to set that to music, a decision Maeterlinck would eventually come to regret. *Pelléas,* Debussy's only completed opera, was to occupy the composer for ten years before its 1902 premiere. Other works of the late 1880s and early 1890s include *Roderigue et Chimène,* an opera Debussy almost finished; songs based on poetry by Baudelaire, Verlaine, and texts by the composer; the *Deux arabesques* for piano; and sketches for the *Suite bergamasque* and the three *Nocturnes* for orchestra. The 1889 *Fantaisie* for piano and orchestra, a concerto in all but name, is his only surviving excursion into a developmental, conflict-driven form he would from then avoid.

Finding his given name Achille-Claude pretentious, Debussy around this time reversed them to the more familiar Claude-Achille. He made friends with the eccentric composer Erik Satie, with whom he would stay close for the rest of his life, and the talented Ernest Chausson. Debussy was also friends during these years with Paul Dukas, composer of *The Sorcerer's Apprentice.* Debussy moved in with Gaby Dupont, a strong-willed woman who served as the young composer's part-time mistress and manager. The nature of their relationship remains murky, however: he had many affairs for the eight or so years they shared apartments and was even engaged to someone else briefly in 1893. Some of the mistresses Dupont seems blithely to have ignored, while others were inexplicably the cause of ugly scenes. Debussy, whose fame if not his unusual looks made him attractive, was to marry twice. He seems to have had plenty of affairs throughout his life.

Photographs of Debussy (some more than others) reveal a man with strange protrusions on his forehead, causing that feature to resemble a cliff or the prow of a ship. The head itself seems to have been quite large, framed by thick, wavy, dark brown hair. He had a straight nose and large, deep-set eyes; his young friend Igor Stravinsky noted that his daughter Chouchou had teeth "like tusks" that resembled his (qtd. in Nichols, *Life* 127). His voice is described by a student as "slightly nasal" (qtd. in Nichols, *Life* 90). Unlike his father, he seems to have been apathetic about politics, uninterested even by the Dreyfus affair, which split France into progressive and reactionary factions in the years around the turn of the twentieth century. He smoked heavily and liked to eat and drink well; he was apparently an excellent cook, but a poor tennis player and worse money manager. Debussy is described as a *"grand enfant"*—a big kid (qtd. in Nichols, *Life* 147). Certainly he is at his most conventionally appealing in his relationship with Chouchou, whom he adored unstintingly. By all accounts this extraordinary artist was a shy, guarded, blunt, prickly man.

The final years of the nineteenth century were productive if difficult for Debussy: most of his time was spent on *Pelléas,* but he also worked intensively on the *Nocturnes* for orchestra, the *Pour le piano* suite, and the *Chansons de Bilitis,* three exquisite songs on texts by his friend Pierre Louÿs. Despite a generous subsidy from the publisher Georges Hartmann, Debussy's finances bottomed out in 1898, as they would again several times, despite fame and regular performances of his music. His spendthrift ways, combined with the fact that he published few works during these years, and the consequent infrequency of performances of his music, probably squeezed his income to a trickle. He made some money as a pianist, notably in workshop performances of Wagner operas. Yet somehow his finances seem not to have improved, even after the 1902 premiere of *Pelléas* and the steadier flow of masterworks afterward.

On October 19, 1899, Debussy married Lily Texier, a model and seamstress for a fashionable dressmaker. The marriage soon became unhappy for both, especially after he took up with the wealthy singer Emma Bardac in 1904. Worldly, strong-willed, and musically sophisticated, Bardac was a better match for Debussy than the attractive but simple Texier, although he and Bardac were to have their share of difficulties, too. It is known that Debussy told Lily that he was leaving her and that she threatened suicide, which she finally attempted by shooting herself in the breast on October 13, 1904 (Nichols, *Life*. 114). He pressed on with the divorce, as did Bardac with her husband. A scandal ensued in which many of the composer's friends turned on him for what they saw as his outrageous treatment of Texier, who survived her wound. Debussy and Bardac were not to marry until January 1908; it is unclear why they waited, but their daughter Claude-Emma—Chouchou—was born on October 10, 1905.

As with many artists, the time of Debussy's greatest personal travails were also among his most creative, with no hint of his misery showing through in his work. In the years before and after 1900, Debussy composed many of his best-known works. In addition to completing *Pelléas et Mélisande,* which received its premiere in 1902, he finished the *Nocturnes* for orchestra in 1899, and the mighty *La mer* between 1903 and 1905. He also wrote some of his greatest music for piano, closing out his early style with the *Suite bergamasque* (begun in 1890) in 1905, taking a more radical approach in *Pour le piano* of 1901, and finally gaining his completely individual aesthetic with the revolutionary *Estampes* of 1903.

The premiere of *Pelléas* in at the Opéra-Comique in Paris in the spring of 1902 was fraught with scandals and production problems. For several reasons the playwright Maeterlinck came to oppose the project, developing an undying enmity toward Debussy and his opera. But despite a number of disruptions by the audience (which probably stimulated interest in the opera) and mixed reviews from critics, the reactionary half of whom predictably found the work puzzling, there was enormous curiosity about it, and subsequent performances that season were well attended. Debussy was awarded the Croix d'Honneur, a government medal, making his father proud (Nichols, *Life* 108–9).

In 1901, Debussy began to write performance reviews and columns for *La revue blanche,* a liberal journal covering politics and the arts. Over the years, he contributed to several other publications, continuing to write almost to the end of his life. Debussy was a clever, insightful critic, never shy of phrasemongering. His witticisms were far ranging. Some of his most trenchant comments were reserved for his onetime idol Wagner. With supreme insight and verbal grace, Debussy likened Wagner to "a beautiful sunset that has been mistaken for a sunrise" (Lesure 83). More acidly, he called a piece by the English composer Frederick Delius "very sweet, very pale—music to soothe convalescents in well-to-do neighborhoods" (Lesure 16–17). Clearly pleased with this trope, he used it again two years later in a review of some songs by Edvard Grieg, then proceeded to mock the Norwegian composer's appearance, offending him deeply. Those intrigued by this side of Debussy's career would do well to read his reviews and essays, collected in *Debussy on Music,* edited by François Lesure. Although many of the reviews are of forgotten music played by forgotten artists, Debussy's writings offer an invaluable glimpse of his sharp mind and pen.

The years from the turn of the century until around 1915, when illness and a sense of mortality altered Debussy's style, were some of his most productive. *La mer,* that paradigm of oceanic fluidity and power, had its premiere on October 15, 1905, and despite a few foolish complaints that the work didn't evoke the sea at all, sensible, sensitive critics and listeners found Debussy's mastery clear and undeniable. The composer quietly worked on some of the greatest music of this, his middle period, publishing the first set of *Images* for piano in 1905 and starting work on the orchestral pieces of the same title the following year. He also toyed with ideas for another opera, but none of these were carried through. That year also saw the publication of the composer's second set of *Images* for piano and continued labor on the *Images* for orchestra.

Now famous across Europe and the United States and in demand as a conductor of his own works, Debussy began to tour: in 1908 and 1909 he was in London to conduct the *Prélude à l'après-midi d'un faune* and the *Nocturnes.* In 1910 he wrote the first book of preludes for piano, one of the landmarks of the keyboard literature, and traveled to Vienna and

Budapest. In Vienna he complained, in a letter to his wife, of a violist in the Konzertverein orchestra who refused to play his music and stared at him "as though he were in a shop-window" (qtd. in Nichols, *Life* 135). He loved, however, hearing gypsy fiddlers in the cafés (ibid.). It was also around this time that Debussy began to suffer from the earliest symptoms of the rectal cancer that killed him in 1918.

In 1911, Debussy began the second book of preludes for piano, while hurrying to produce the sprawling sacred drama *Le martyre de St Sébastien*. It marked for Debussy the first step into a third, more dense and spiritual style, which he expressed with ever-greater clarity as his time ran out. Nineteen-twelve saw the creation of the ballet *Jeux* (Games), a masterful score that combines density with weightlessness, composed for the Russian dancer and choreographer Vaslav Nijinsky. The descent of *Jeux* from the *Prélude à l'après-midi d'un faune* of nineteen years earlier is apparent, as is the expansion in the composer's depth, range, and subtlety. Appreciation for this work has widened over the decades but still seems limited chiefly to musicians—who adore it—and to sophisticated listeners. He also began to compose *Khamma*, another ballet, which he would finish but never orchestrate.

Debussy's acquaintance with the young Igor Stravinsky dated to the younger composer's time in Paris beginning around 1912. Debussy recognized Stravinsky's gift and sensed in him a fellow radical, and the two great musical revolutionaries of successive generations grew close. Debussy admired Stravinsky's wonderful ballet score *Petrushka* of 1911, the influence of which can be heard in the percussive rhythms and bright, brittle harmonies of some of the etudes and in the two-piano suite *En blanc et noir*. In June 1912, Debussy played portions of Stravinsky's *Le sacre du printemps* (The Rite of Spring) with the composer. This score, which caused riots at its Paris premiere the next year, is one of the most famous works in musical history, definitively marking the birth of the modern. Although *Le sacre du printemps* disturbed Debussy as it did everyone, he wrote of it as "a beautiful nightmare" (qtd. in Nichols, *Life* 141). The usually acerbic Stravinsky wrote fondly of Debussy in his autobiography, admiring his piano playing, noting:

> I was seeing a good deal of Debussy, and was deeply touched by his
> sympathetic attitude towards me and my music. I was struck by
> the delicacy of his appreciation, and was grateful to him, among
> other things, for having observed what so few had then noticed.
> (Stravinsky 57)

A planned trip to Boston in 1913 could not be undertaken because of Emma Debussy's refusal to travel, but the composer did go to Russia in December of that year. Musically the visit, his first since his travels as Madame von Meck's house pianist thirty years earlier, went very well. Twenty famous Russian musicians wrote him a letter of thanks, but his wife's letters, which have not survived but must have been filled with complaints, made his life miserable. The tours of 1914 to Italy, Holland, and Belgium, which might have been triumphal, seem to have been only wearing to the composer, who in all fairness was ill and worried about the onset of war. As with many artists, the manic energy Debussy needed in order to create was balanced with heavy depressions.

It was at this time that his publisher, Jacques Durand, asked him to edit the works of Chopin for publication. While the start of World War I in August drew Debussy's full, anxious attention, he must on another level have been digesting the glories of Chopin, always one of his musical idols. In a final, magnificent burst of creativity, Debussy composed the twelve etudes for piano, dedicated to the Polish master's memory, as well as *En blanc et noir,* and he began the three chamber sonatas that were to be his final works. In these remarkable late works, the spirituality that had begun to manifest itself a few years earlier can be heard in full flower. It is impossible not to sense in this desperately beautiful, often unearthly music the meditations of a great spirit coming to grips with mortality.

In late 1915, Debussy underwent an operation, which, given the primitive treatments then available for cancer, must have been agonizing and was sure to fail, as well. He watched the devastations of the war with immense grief but found his patriotism stimulated. On the title page of the three chamber sonatas, he added after his name the words *"musicien français."* With much effort, Debussy completed his last work, the Sonata for Violin and Piano, in early 1917; he also played in public

for the last time at its premiere on May 5 of that year. By the beginning
of 1918, Debussy was bedridden. He died late in the evening of March
25, to the sound of German artillery bombarding Paris. He was buried
first at the Père-Lachaise cemetery, where Chopin is interred, but was
later moved to the graveyard at Passy. His widow, Emma, died in 1934.
As a sad postscript, his beloved daughter Chouchou died of diphtheria
in the summer of 1919, a few months shy of her fourteenth birthday.
By all odds, Chouchou was Debussy's great love.

The Music for Orchestra, 1887–99

The division of the orchestral works into those Debussy composed before and after the turn of the twentieth century is more or less arbitrary. His most important scores for orchestra, the *Prélude à l'après-midi d'un faune* (1892–94), the *Nocturnes* (1893–99), *La mer* (1903–5), the *Images* (1906–12), and *Jeux* (1912), form a steady stylistic progression. There are, however, flaws in such a conception: though early, the *Prélude* is as great as anything that follows, and, though perhaps falling just short of the stature of the later works, the *Nocturnes* clearly anticipate the other three-part symphonic suites *La mer* and *Images* in form and scope. The date is merely a convenient dividing line, with Debussy's orchestral works from the *Prélude à l'après-midi d'un faune* being uniformly stunning in content and technical finish.

Printemps (Spring) is the earliest of Debussy's works that is regularly performed, although it is more readily encountered on recordings than in the concert hall. He composed the two-movement symphonic poem in 1887 as a Prix de Rome requirement in a lost version for chorus and orchestra; the one played today, without chorus, was executed in 1913 by the conductor Henri Busser under the composer's supervision. *Printemps* shows remarkably little of the direction Debussy was to follow or of the stature he would achieve but makes for pleasant listening on its own. While *Printemps* is far from great, it grows on the listener.

In *Printemps,* the music moves in a steady upward arc from the still opening of the first movement to the triumphal dance that ends the second. The opening describes in a nonspecific way—without birdcalls or gurgling brooks—a slow awakening from wintry rigor. What follows is tender, sweet, and charming, somewhat reminiscent of the music of

Massenet; one might discern, in the muted horn calls, anticipations of the *Prélude à l'après-midi d'un faune*. A falling chromatic scale late in the movement feels forced, laid on from the outside rather than generated by the music's expressive flow. Following an introductory section that features some bright instrumental coloring, the body of the second movement is driven by a swaggering tune of a sort Debussy would not employ again without irony. Sounding a bit like a high-class film score, it builds to a brassy, choreographic climax.

With the masterpieces of 1892–94, Debussy's genius seems to explode. The tightly structured String Quartet of 1893 shows his severe Apollonian side, and the *Prélude à l'après-midi d'un faune* (track 1 on the CD at the back of the book) displays his highly charged sensuality, which is, however, flawlessly melded to its expressive vehicle. Perfection of message and means has earned for the *Prélude* enduring and well-deserved popularity with audiences and the nearly universal admiration of professional musicians.

The *Prélude* is loosely based on the symbolist poet Stéphane Mallarmé's dramatic monologue *L'après-midi d'un faune* (The Afternoon of a Faun), which attempts to express the thoughts and desires on a hot day of a lustful faun of classical Greek mythology. Half man, half goat, the faun recalls in juicy detail the pair of nymphs he nearly seduced earlier; slow and heavy in the heat of his native Sicily, he then ponders the reed pipes he makes and plays, and reflects on the seductive magic of music. Overripe, a bit overwrought, and on the long side, this mediation on sex and art is an artifact of an extinct aesthetic that can make for heavy reading today.

Debussy saw no need to follow Mallarmé's text literally, however. Instead, he takes his own impression of the poem, transcribing it into a score of matchless richness, density, and beauty. Where Mallarmé is prolix, Debussy is pithy: the poem seems long to read, but the ten-minute tone poem is over in a flash. Debussy's sole concession to Mallarmé is his recurring use of the flute to evoke the faun's reed pipe, but even this tone painting is far broader and deeper than the poet's imagery. Debussy's British biographer Edward Lockspeiser speculates (183–84) that the music may have originated in a lost Prix de Rome offering of 1884, about which one of the composer's instructors commented, "All this is very interesting, but you must keep it for later" (184). But this was guesswork; besides, the material of the *Prélude* and its highly polished technique mark bold advances from anything the composer had done before.

While it might be an overstatement to call them friends, the poet and composer knew each other well. Debussy played the *Prélude* for Mallarmé on the piano, then invited him to its premiere in December 1894. Sensitive to music and a believer in the unity of all the arts, Mallarmé seems to have liked the work, writing afterward to Debussy that it was an "illustration which would present no dissonance with my text. Rather does it go much further into the nostalgia and light with subtlety, malaise, and richness" (qtd. in Lockspeiser 185).

The work opens with a famous flute solo, the languid, dreamy character of which places it in opposition to the emphatic themes, ripe for development, typical of a German sonata-style movement. This melody droops, pauses, rises, pauses again, then falls and pauses once more before rising to its high point at 0:14. At 0:20, as the flute pauses, the oboes, clarinets, and one horn enter gently, playing a sweetly dissonant chord, backed by a harp glissando. Careful instrumentation of a chamber-music-like delicacy is a hallmark of the *Prélude* from start to finish, with countless hidden felicities of instrumental combinations revealing themselves on repeated hearings of the work. The opening sequence ends in hesitating phrases (0:23) for two horns. Evoking the silence from which the music seemed to emerge, there is a long pause; then (0:30) the violins pick up the chords that the winds first played, with another harp run as the horns resume their murmuring dialogue. At 0:44, over trembling strings and horns, the flute repeats the opening theme, which is, however, taken over and extended by the oboe (1:02).

Now (1:17) the violins take up an impassioned extension of the oboe's tune amid the thickest orchestral texture Debussy has yet deployed, which, however, maintains its transparency. This theme plays itself out in a graceful phrase for the clarinets (1:26); with the pauses, hesitations, and long silences, what one hears seems like one vast melodic phrase, an impression that Debussy miraculously carries through the length of the work. The opening theme returns, breaking into roulades at 1:42 over more animated figures on the harp. The strings come in delicately beneath, as the second flute joins the first in a dialogue that is playful and passionate.

At 2:50, above a shuddering figure for the cellos, the clarinet takes on the chief role, playing the rolling theme with, off, and against the flute. It is easy to hear the buzzing and to picture the movement of insects in the hot sun as the woodwind lines roll gracefully above waltz-like chords on the harp. The tune for oboe that appears at 3:16, strongest yet in melodic rhythmic and melodic profiles, seems to grow organically from what went before, as does its passionate extension in the violins (3:26). The animation of tempo and abrupt change of key at 3:40 would surely signal a climax in a more conventional work, but instead, the winds and horns engage in a dialogue that is at first playful but gradually loses steam in a gorgeous phrase at 3:55 for the horns, followed by a change of key and a long, languid clarinet solo (4:08) based on the rhythm of the strong oboe melody.

As this tune plays itself out, it melts into a broad melody (proving once and for all that Debussy was a great melodist in the conventional sense) for all the winds over throbbing strings. Now, without growing stormy, the music achieves its most intense passion, as the winds play elaborated versions of the theme (4:48) and the strings sing out their glorious melody, and winds and harps take on the accompanying role, which in this case consists of triplets broken into heaving, panting fragments (4:56). The ornamentations of the theme are as significant as the melodic line itself, and while sumptuously scored, a fine performance of this passage, like the one on the CD, will maintain utter clarity for every instrument.

At 5:24, Debussy begins to thin the texture, breaking it into melodic and ornamental fragments played at 5:35 by horns, then clarinets, then oboes (5:47), all to the accompaniment of a solo violin. Building tension again (5:57), Debussy changes key suddenly, as the flute plays an augmented version of the opening theme over streaming arpeggios for the harp. This thematic incarnation is interrupted at 6:14 by another abrupt key change and sparkling, playful downward figures for the winds over shivering strings (6:21). The opening flute melody over the harp recurs solemnly at 6:28, followed at 6:43 by more playful figuration for horns and winds, here accompanied by plucked strings and harp.

The *Prélude* begins to move with languid grace toward its conclusion. The flutes play the opening theme over shuddering strings (7:00) as two violins play the oboe theme (7:08). In one of Debussy's great inspirations of scoring, antique cymbals chime in; they will be heard now through to the end. Flutes and oboes softly play the impassioned roulades as violins, then the muted horns sing out a broad phrase based on the climactic melody. At 7:33, a solo cello receives the privilege of chanting the main theme with the flutes, which it does touchingly, as the harps comment.

The closing pages are perhaps the most magical of all. Accompanied by oboe and English horn, the flutes play a strange, rhythmically altered version of their melody (7:51) as the oboe picks up the tail of the first theme (8:00); the violins chant the even rhythm of the oboe tune, here barely recognizable. Preceded by out-of-rhythm harps (8:17), the horns, in an unforgettable muted phrase, play the opening theme (8:24), which the listener perceives as though from a vast distance in space, or perhaps memory. Flutes, violins, harps, and the exquisite antique cymbals reach upward one last, languid time, as the gently plucked chords of the cellos and basses end the work; sensitive listeners may hear a silence, like that from which the music arose, that follows.

The sensuous beauty of the music, its ceaseless lyric flow, the listener's continual delight in its ever-changing instrumental color ensure that no dry listing of the highlights of the *Prélude à l'après-midi d'un faune* will capture its uncanny aural depiction of desire on a hot summer day. But it is Debussy's skill at picturing the faun's consciousness as his mind flits between the music of his pipe to lust, with a fair number of distractions along the way, that is the source of the work's truest and deepest greatness. With music deepening the sense of words, Debussy uses Mallarmé's poem as a springboard for his own insights. The faun, symbolizing man's carnal nature, broods almost constantly about sex, as his art—his work—in the form of the music of the flute, runs as an obbligato to his erotic musings. The two streams separate, run together, then separate again, with the mind constantly drawn away by insects and birds on the wing, as well as other, nameless diversions.

One of the great paradoxes of Debussy's art is that he had to impose on himself the most rigorous concentration to depict in it the random motions of the mind and its inability to relax. Seeking a deeper layer, he did not try to describe the conventional emotion of love, but rather the lustful instincts that lie beneath. In the *Prélude* he also probes at the connection between that procreative instinct and the need of the artist, in the guise of the music-making faun, to create. Debussy was perhaps the supreme master in Western music at picturing the familiar but frustratingly mysterious workings of the mind: the *Prélude à l'après-midi d'un faune,* his first masterpiece and one of his most wonderful, represents his explosive entry into the realm of musical psychology.

In 1912 the Russian dancer and choreographer Vaslav Nijinsky choreographed the *Prélude* score for performances in Paris. Taking the role of the faun himself, Nijinsky ended his version by masturbating against a veil dropped by one of the nymphs. A scandal ensued, with police in attendance for the second performance. Debussy hated the angularity of the choreography, which surely went against the grain of this most fluid score, as well as its explicitness (Nichols, *Life* 141). The eroticism of the music was clear to the dancer, but not its repression.

A letter written by Debussy in 1894 to the eminent Belgian violinist Eugène Ysaÿe refers to the *Nocturnes* as being for solo violin and orchestra; two years later, he flatteringly asked the violinist to perform the solo part. But in 1897, Debussy reconceived the works without the violin solo, of which in the final version there is, indeed, not a hint. This change engendered no ill will between composer and Ysaÿe, who conducted them several years later in Brussels. Two of the three movements were performed in Paris in 1897, then again in 1900, omitting the third movement, *Sirènes,* for lack of a female chorus; the first complete performance occurred in 1901. The works were well received by the avant-garde from the start. The young Maurice Ravel attended a performance and wrote with admiration of Debussy's new work, and he transcribed *Sirènes* for two pianos.

The *Nocturnes* are not "night pieces" like Chopin's. They are instead visually inspired studies in tonal and orchestral color, interspersed with dreamlike moments. Debussy himself wrote:

> The title *Nocturnes* is to be interpreted here in a general and, more particularly, in a decorative sense. Therefore it is not meant to designate the usual form of the nocturne, but rather all the various impressions and the special effects of light that the word suggests. *Nuages* renders the immutable aspect of the sky and the slow, solemn motion of the clouds, fading away in grey tones lightly tinged with white. *Fêtes* gives us the vibrating atmosphere with sudden flashes of light . . . *Sirènes* depicts the sea and its countless rhythms. (qtd. in Lockspeiser 189)

The opening movement, *Nuages* (Clouds) evokes a shifting cloudscape with remarkable success. Playing in a soft, even rhythm, the woodwinds paint an unmistakable image, through which the plaintive, nasal sound of an English horn cuts, like a change of light in the clouds. The strings eerily assume the even, drifting figure, cut again by the slightly sharper figure of the English horn. About two minutes in, the oboes, clarinets, and bassoons, playing in their lower registers, chant a somber, rising melody that suggests a thickening of the clouds; plucked strings shortly afterward capture the feeling of fractured light. This solemn woodwind tune assumes yet another incarnation with flute and harp singing above motionless strings.

Nuages is hauntingly beautiful music from first note to last, but it is not easy; its countless inspirations reveal themselves only with repeated, sympathetic listening. As with the *Prélude à l'après-midi d'un faune,* Debussy's orchestration is exquisite, though more austere than in the earlier work. And, although *Nuages* has no conventional, old-fashioned melodies, the entire movement has an unmistakable lyrical flow not unlike that of the *Prélude;* thus had Debussy's craft marvelously evolved. Comparing *Nuages* with *Fêtes,* his friend, the fine composer Paul Dukas, of *The Sorcerer's Apprentice,* wrote that he preferred the former, because in it "the art that truly belongs to M. Debussy appears to me there more distinctly drawn" (qtd. in Nichols, *Life* 99).

Fêtes (Holidays) provides the greatest contrast imaginable with *Nuages.* Moving always at a breathless pace, it opens with a fierce rhythmic proclamation by the violins, followed by a slithering figure for the winds. The heavy brass interrupt, followed by a sweep of the harps, before the opening figure returns, now suggesting a cheerful throng determined to have a good time. The music stops, and the harps throb in march rhythm as the trumpets play a series of faraway fanfares that clearly depict an approaching parade or procession. But here, for all its brilliance, the music has that remote, removed quality of the mature Debussy painting a musical picture. While painting the scene, he is not in or of it but somehow above, apart. There may be reminiscences in this dreamlike sequence of the mock trumpet calls above a thundering bass line in the middle section of Liszt's great piano work *Funérailles,* which itself echoes the central episode of Chopin's "Heroic" Polonaise, op. 53.

Debussy drives his carefully controlled march and fanfares to a tumult. But the commotion dies down suddenly as the slithering figure returns in the flutes, now reincarnated as a waltz, over chattering lower winds; this waltz plays itself out in a Bacchic frenzy, which also loses steam, then peters out, like any dance that begins in wild excitement but ends in exhaustion. The wild waltz expresses its depletion with muted trumpets, as though the dance lingers wearily in memory, and then breaks apart in the tympani and low strings. Here again, Debussy finds and paints with music the simple, essential human experience of the holiday festival anticipated, lived through with barely contained excitement, and concluded in fatigue. *Fêtes* is a superb example of Debussy's ability to compose music about music, with the march and the waltz that approach, rage in excitement, then expire.

The sirens of the third movement of *Fêtes* are the dangerous demi-goddesses of the *Odyssey,* who lured sailors to their deaths on the rocky shore of their island with the irresistible beauty of their song. As Debussy wrote, the music is oceanic in nature; a female chorus singing wordless vowels—toward the end with their mouths closed, in a strange and haunting effect—stands in for the sirens. Ravel admired this technique, employing it to similarly superb effect in his 1912 ballet *Daphnis et Chloé,* also based on Greek mythology. The rocking motion of the strings and the gurgling of the woodwinds, interspersed with the metallic flash of the trumpet, capture the feel of the sea with accuracy and magnificence; the sweeping lines of the wordless chorus may seem odd at first but work better at each hearing. *Sirènes*'s only flaw is simply that it is a bit less powerful than *La mer,* its immense descendant of several years later. Far too grand to be regarded as merely a sketch for the later work, however, *Sirènes* stands entirely on its own merits.

The advance Debussy made in content and refinement of technique between *Printemps* and the *Prélude à l'après-midi d'un faune* is geometric, exponential; from then on his orchestral thinking grew in refinement and power, albeit in more measured steps.

Pour le Piano I:
The Early Works for Keyboard

D ebussy's mastery is already apparent in the songs of the early
1880s, but these are not widely known or appreciated. The
compositions he created for the piano between 1888 and 1901,
however, include works of beauty and charm that have achieved wide
and apparently undying popularity. While his later piano works are,
without exception, greater, these early pieces point clearly toward those
he composed after 1903.

It is easy to find in Debussy's early piano music the ideas, formal
and thematic, that the composer would develop with greater eloquence
and depth in the later keyboard works. The suites of short pieces the
composer would later assemble into groups of three or twelve, all
roughly equal in length and weight, had not yet gelled, with the opening
sections of both the *Suite bergamasque* and *Pour le piano* being longer
than what follows. The sweeping arpeggios of the *Prélude* of the *Suite
bergamasque* look forward to those of the opening movement of *Pour le
piano;* in the final movement of the latter, anticipations of the rhythmically alert perpetual-motion pieces that end *Estampes* and both sets
of *Images* can be heard. The formal outlines, as well as the melancholy
and ecstasy of *Hommage à Rameau* (track 7 on the CD) of the first set
of *Images* is readily discerned in the *Sarabande* of *Pour le piano*. These
early pieces were, however, mostly composed before or as Debussy
developed his pictorial style. As a result, many of the early works have
abstract, formal titles adopted by the composer from his idols of the
baroque era, rather than the descriptive names that dominate from the
Estampes of 1903 on.

Some of the early works inspired directly by Chopin are slight. The *Ballade* of 1890 is a slender, flowing work with none of the titanic scope of Chopin's four masterworks of the same title; the *Nocturne* of the same year, although written in D-flat major, one of the Polish master's favorite keys, is also negligible. The bouncy little *Mazurka* of the following year is a clever take on Chopin's great dances, but without their profundity. The two *Arabesques* of 1888, three-part pieces resembling Chopin's impromptus, have more to offer. The first, a sweet but polished study in arpeggios, has achieved a sort of contemporary fame as a musical cell-phone ring; its more playful companion opens with buzzing triplets and features a chordal middle section before the reprise of the opening.

The most substantial of Debussy's keyboard works before the *Suite bergamasque* is the *Danse* of 1890. Originally known as the *Tarantelle styrienne,* the *Danse* is a work of beauty, dimension, and a kind of open joyousness that is rare in Debussy's emotionally veiled oeuvre. The piece opens with a statement of the excited primary melody in the left hand beneath chords in the right that suggest the strumming of a guitar. The second appearance of the melody is in loud octaves in the right hand, upheld by chattering chords in the left. Gently lilting melodic fragments appear that foreshadow the tarantella heard in the distance in *Les collines d'Anacapri* from the first set of *Préludes* (track 8 on the CD). Surely inspired by Chopin's Scherzo no. 4, the brief but musically spacious middle section shows Debussy's ability to apply his profound grasp of that master to his own works with complete originality and success. Some of the dry harmonies in this section also show Debussy's own influence on Ravel, who in 1925 orchestrated the *Danse*. This immensely likable piece ends on a triumphant statement of the main theme trailed by a flashing arpeggio.

Debussy composed the *Suite bergamasque* in 1889 or 1890 but did not publish it until 1905, when the composer's newfound fame inspired his publisher to press for new music to sell. Debussy revised the *Suite* (apparently unhappily) just before it was published. It is a fine work in all respects, although by 1905 the composer had moved far from its nostalgic style into brave new realms. The word *bergamasque* refers to the rough Italian street theater known as *commedia dell'arte,* which features puppets playing stock characters including Pulcinella, Scaramouche, Pierrot, and Arlequin, with Punch and Judy their English-language descendants. There is little further reference to *commedia dell'arte* in the music, however, which is instead a look back at musical structures and affects of the eighteenth century.

The opening *Prélude* begins with a grand gesture reminiscent of the parallel movements in countless keyboard suites by Couperin, Rameau, and the other *clavecinistes,* as well as Bach in his seven partitas. The music has a fine bustle and a hint of comic pomposity. In imitation of his baroque models, Debussy has demure, "feminine" musical phrases reply to more aggressive "masculine" ones; there is also an oft-repeated turn in quick notes that is typical of the old style. There is just a hint of stiffness in the phrasing that seems to be part of Debussy's plan but that he would scrupulously avoid in later works. But this is extremely original, charming music that has real depth, as well. A playfully dry *Menuet* follows. Its influence on Ravel, the exquisite minuet of whose 1917 piano suite *Le tombeau de Couperin* echoes it quite clearly, was considerable. Near the end of this ironic dance is a passionate outburst that seems to rise through the keys before vanishing in a comic rhythm and a long scale.

The third movement, *Clair de lune,* has long been Debussy's most famous piece. While below the composer at his mature peak, *Clair de lune* has much merit and is undeniably very beautiful. Debussy's admirers have pointed out repeatedly that it has "dampened curiosity among the uninitiate concerning any of the composer's subsequent works" (Lockspeiser 145); but also that "the extraordinary popularity obtained by this composition should not induce the musician to underrate its importance" (Schmitz 53). The title, which means nothing more than "moonlight," shows *Clair de lune* to be one of the composer's earliest attempts at pictorial music.

The famous, drooping, wistful phrase that opens *Clair de lune* conceals considerable art. An unusual time signature tells the pianist that long, graceful phrasing is required, and the pacing has a spaciousness that reflects Debussy's intimate knowledge of Chopin, another master of short works that are ripe with emotion. A passionate chordal phrase follows, then four gorgeous broken chords, leading into the sweeping middle section, the arpeggios of which seem to say that the moonlight of this musical image is reflected in water. The opening phrase returns, rendered over more fluid arpeggios, then stated plainly before a final rippling sequence brings this fine-boned nocturne to a dreamy close.

With the *Passepied,* Debussy follows the convention of ending an instrumental suite with a lively dance movement. This one originated in the coastal French province of Brittany; the other famous example of a passepied is the last movement of Bach's first Suite for Orchestra. Debussy's is almost prickly, its nature growing out of the tart harmony and the crisp, steady rhythm of the left hand. There are a couple of lyrical phrases that pass quickly, and a magical conclusion. The feel of the *Passepied* somewhat resembles that of the second-movement minuet, but it is more emotionally contained and its tone far more earnest. In fact, the deepening seriousness of tone as the *Suite bergamasque* progresses leaves an impression of a solid, serious effort by the young composer.

Seriousness, intensity, and brilliance are the characteristics of *Pour le piano,* the three-movement suite begun by Debussy in 1896 and completed in 1901. The opening *Prélude* is an agitated perpetual motion in fast notes leading to a huge, Stravinskian climax on heavily accented chords and dazzling *glissandi*—those fast slides of notes the pianist creates by running the fingers along the keys. Throughout this very difficult movement, the music expresses a burning urgency far removed from the geniality of its opposite number in the *Suite bergamasque.* The big climax returns, followed by a wild passage of real grandeur that leads into a cadenza—a sequence of brilliant flourishes that is more playful. Six grand chords conclude this remarkable movement.

Looking backward again for his form, the second movement of *Pour le piano* is a sarabande, a stately triple-meter dance with roots in Spain and possibly the Middle East. Bach used the sarabande as the center of gravity in the suites for solo cello, the partitas for keyboard, and two of the three partitas for solo violin; Couperin and Rameau, whom Debussy revered as his musical ancestors, also composed their share. Debussy marked that this one is to be played "with a slow and grave elegance." And indeed, this majestic piece is filled with profound emotion that is reined in and veiled in the composer's typical way. The main theme features masses of chastely billowing chords in a keyboard sound he loved and was to use many times. A thinning of texture in the proclamatory middle section shows Debussy's absolute grasp of Chopin's textures and techniques, recalling the rocking movements in that composer's Ballade no. 4 and *Barcarolle.* In addition to the obvious ancestry of this piece to *Hommage à Rameau,* the powerful sarabande that is the second of *Images I,* it also anticipates moments in the stately, sarabande-like prelude *Danseuses de Delphes.*

The bustling *Toccata* that concludes the suite maintains the seriousness of the work, while providing emotional release, first in gorgeous chords over sweeping arpeggios. A section follows in which the left hand is called on to imitate trumpet calls, as it will later in *En blanc et noir* for two pianos. There is a change near the end to an unusual key (C-sharp major), and a sense of triumph that is, however, hard-won. The big chords at the very end echo those that concluded the opening movement of the suite. With its sense of struggle and passion, this splendid piece is the direct ancestor of the toccata that ends Ravel's *Le tombeau de Couperin*—a movement that, however, stands squarely on its own merits. *Pour le piano* is the culminating masterpiece of Debussy's early keyboard style, approaching *Estampes* in its intensity while falling just short of that work's revolutionary formal freedom and boldness of piano sonority.

There is one more set of important piano works from the early period: the three pieces composed in 1894—but not published until 1978—under the title *Images.* It is unclear why Debussy did not publish this forward-looking set, as it is superior musically to the *Suite bergamasque.* Equally uncertain is why this beautiful stepchild is never heard today. The fine pianist Paul Jacobs, who died in 1983, recorded it in the year of its publication. His beautiful performance remains in the catalogue and qualifies as a must-buy.

This superb set consists of a slow, sad opening movement, reminiscent in mood of the contemporaneous *Pelléas et Mélisande;* the somber repeated chords just after the opening were to continue as a magnificent element in his imagination for years. The second movement of *Images* is another version of the sarabande at the center of *Pour le piano,* with which the similarities far outweigh the differences. The final piece, titled "*Quelques aspects de 'Nous n'irons pas au bois ...'*" plays on a nursery song that Debussy used several times, most notably in *Jardins sous la pluie,* the third piece of *Estampes.* Another frisky finger study, this lighthearted music contrasts well with the melancholy seriousness of what went before. A quotation from *Boris Godunov* near the end demonstrates Debussy's devotion to that masterpiece.

The Great Opera

ike Beethoven, Debussy completed only a single opera, and the former's *Fidelio* and the latter's *Pelléas et Mélisande* stand as perhaps the two most individual members of the elite operatic repertory. Like Beethoven, Debussy struggled for years with his score, revising it over and over, right up to and even after its premiere. And, like *le vieux sourd,* Debussy's low productivity in the field was not because of lack of interest: both composers examined operatic possibilities throughout their careers, with Debussy beginning, then putting aside, many operatic projects. In addition to the operatic ideas on which Debussy worked intensively and described in his letters, there may have been more that never saw the light of day.

The other projects about which there is firm information make an exceptionally interesting assortment. Two stories by Edgar Allan Poe, the American writer much admired by the French symbolists of the late nineteenth century, got the most attention. These were *Le diable dans le beffroi,* based on "The Devil in the Belfry," on which Debussy worked starting in 1902 after the premiere of *Pelléas;* second is *La chute de la maison Usher,* based on "The Fall of the House of Usher," begun by Debussy in 1908 and on which he worked for the rest of his life. Le *diable* evidently contained the fascinating idea that the devil would only whistle (Lockspeiser 111); the composer's references to *Usher* in his correspondence suggest great emotion, and it must be a source of regret that, at the height of his powers, he finished neither of the Poe-based projects.

Shakespeare, idol and terror to most opera composers, was the source for *Comme il vous plaira—As You Like It*. This project also closely followed *Pelléas* but was dropped when Debussy's librettist left Paris for southeast Asia. The remaining two abandoned projects are yet more astonishing. With *Orphée-roi* (Orpheus the King), Debussy hoped to throw down the gauntlet against Christoph Willibald Gluck, composer of the revolutionary *Orfeo ed Euridice,* a forerunner of modern opera, which he disliked. (He surely intended no offense to *Orphée aux enfers*—*Orpheus in the Underworld*—by the excellent Jacques Offenbach, a composer Debussy is on record as admiring.)

For shock value, however, neither tops the Tristan project of 1907, the existence of which is known from two of Debussy's letters. According to Léon Vallas, one of Debussy's early biographers, its "episodical character . . . would have been related to the tales of chivalry, and diametrically opposed to the Germanic conception of Wagner" (qtd. in Lockspeiser 108). That Debussy entertained, even if only for a few weeks, the idea of writing an opera based on the Tristan legend is quite incredible. He knew Wagner's colossal *Tristan und Isolde* as well as anyone, and his confidence must have been great indeed if he felt up to treating the subject. The idea of looking at it from a different angle makes nothing but sense, since this was what Debussy had done with *Pelléas et Mélisande,* as its story essentially follows the outlines of the Tristan myth.

The opera Debussy came closest to finishing is *Rodrigue et Chimène,* which he wrestled with from 1890 until the spring of 1893, when he began work on *Pelléas.* Desperate to sink his teeth into a project of substance, the young composer accepted the type of old-fashioned libretto he dreaded, filled with howlers and lusty choruses of soldiers calling for wine. Its author was Catulle Mendès, a ripely pretentious literary man of the generation preceding Debussy's; the incomprehensible plot is based on the legend of El Cid, the medieval Spanish hero. Describing his struggle with *Rodrigue* to a friend, Debussy wrote: "My life is misery and hardship thanks to this opera. Everything about it is wrong for me" (qtd. in Nichols, *Life* 66).

Debussy left the score fairly complete, though not orchestrated. It passed through the possession of pianist Alfred Cortot, then to the New York philanthropist and collector Robert Lehman. In 1987 it was transcribed and reconstituted by the British Debussy scholar Richard

Langham Smith, then skillfully orchestrated in the style of *Pelléas* by the Russian composer Edward Denisov. A recording of this score, with a top-flight cast and the orchestra of the Opéra de Lyon under Kent Nagano, was produced in 1993 and 1994. On the negative side, the text must be ignored completely, and Debussy's music shows an odd lack of Spanish flavor for a future master of the idiom. While little of *Rodrigue et Chimène* has the kind of profile that lodges itself firmly in the listener's memory, the music is reasonably strong nonetheless, with Debussy's early style coming through loud and clear. There is a very beautiful trio for the characters Don Diegue, Hernan, and Bermudo near the beginning of act 2. The hard-to-find recording on the Musifrance label is well worth hearing.

Debussy's interest in Maurice Maeterlinck's play *Pelléas et Mélisande* can be dated with rare precision to May 1893, when he attended a Paris performance of the work, which had been published the year before. Debussy seems to have begun sketching music for it at once. By August, Debussy had received Maeterlinck's permission to set the work to music and make the cuts necessary to turn the script into a libretto, the composer visiting the playwright at his home in Ghent that fall.

Despite Debussy's early enthusiasm, though, the opera turned into his chief project of nearly the next ten years and is the longest and largest in scale of all his works. He appears to have completed his first version of *Pelléas* in August 1895 (Nichols and Smith 37). Revisions continued over the next few years, while the composer began other works. Despite—or perhaps because of—his onetime adulation of Wagner, Debussy scoured his opera for traces of that master's influences: "Certainly my technique (which consists of doing away with all 'techniques') owes nothing to Wagner," he told a journalist in 1902 (qtd. in Nichols and Smith 80). His goal was to create a musical idiom that would allow the characters themselves, rather than Wagner's style of symphonic development, to find and dictate the pace of the drama.

The Opéra-Comique informed Debussy in 1898 that *Pelléas* was accepted "in principle" for production, but it was not until 1901 that the organization began to prepare the opera. Casting was difficult. Hot-tempered but admittedly nonmusical, Maeterlinck had hoped to have his mistress cast as Mélisande; when the role went to Scottish soprano Mary Garden, he threatened Debussy, disavowed the opera, and began a lifetime of bitter complaints about the composer and the work, which he hoped would be an "immediate and resounding flop" (qtd. in Nichols, *Life* 103). The management of the Opéra-Comique demanded revisions and additions to the orchestral interludes, pushing more work onto Debussy, who was still revising the score and even completing the orchestral scoring right up to the end. Fifteen weeks of rehearsal were required for a work so new in its musical substance and style; the conductor, André Messager, was temperamental, too. The composer found the entire experience terribly wearing. Despite the Maeterlinck scandal and catcalls from reactionaries during the open dress rehearsals and at the April 30 premiere, *Pelléas* was greeted with respect and good reviews by sensible, sensitive critics; its reputation has only grown over the century of its existence.

Maeterlinck's play comes from the peak years of the symbolist period; the movement was in decline by the opera's premiere. The symbolists were an elitist group, producing an art that was affected, even precious, and thus doomed to a short life. In symbolist poetry, things stand for something else, with water, for instance, often used to represent death, or sometimes life. Maeterlinck uses it repeatedly in *Pelléas,* and Debussy, whose own fascination with water was manifest, was in sympathy.

The libretto has some fine qualities, chiefly its sharp-eyed treatment of Golaud. Its weak spots, however, can be embarrassing. For example, Mélisande's line *"Je ne suis pas hereuse"* ("I am not happy") after Golaud drags her about by the hair in act 4 drew howls of laughter in 1902. While that reaction no longer occurs, few would deny that the great strengths of *Pelléas et Mélisande* are its score and Debussy's wonderful sensitivity to the text. Despite the vein of silliness, it's a decent libretto, as librettos go; Debussy's cuts produced a shapely, symmetrical drama that inspired him to a sublime score.

The plot is simple: While lost in a forest, Prince Golaud, the middle-aged grandson of old King Arkël of Allemonde, finds Mélisande, young, beautiful, and mysterious, weeping beside a fountain. Although betrothed to another, he takes her back as his bride. Mélisande and Golaud's younger half-brother Pelléas are drawn to each other. Golaud grows suspicious, then wildly jealous; arrangements are made to send Pelléas away. Surprising the lovers at their final tryst, Golaud kills Pelléas, also wounding Mélisande, who dies after giving birth to Golaud's daughter.

The conventionality of this story, as well as its similarity to *Tristan,* seem obvious; note also Maeterlinck's name for the kingdom: Allemonde, a blend of French and English meaning "all the world," by which he beats his audience over the head with his ambitions for the play's universality. But Debussy's music brings Maeterlinck's story to life and makes the characters breathe. His stern refusal to overstate anything with his music makes *Pelléas* puzzling the first few times one hears or sees it. It is actually the foundation of the work's greatness: Debussy sets the text austerely, one note to a syllable, with the emotional expression mostly to be found in the orchestral underpinning.

Debussy employs the *leitmotiv,* or "leading motif," brought to ripeness and used most systematically by Wagner, but there is little resemblance in the way the two composers went about it. Debussy's themes are less distinctive in profile than Wagner's, Debussy having grown to dislike the German's compulsive use (or abuse) of his leitmotivs. Debussy employs his to set the mood rather than as announcements the listener expects every time its character appears or situation comes up.

The opera opens quietly in the low strings with a slow, compact, profoundly sad thematic figure with a legendary and archaic tone that is also associated, throughout the first scene, with the forest where it is set. The more energetic but still restrained theme associated with Golaud follows, although Debussy finds other uses for it, too. A more flowing, plaintive theme is played by the oboe, high in its register; this is Mélisande's leitmotif. Golaud enters, with his first line, "I shall never get out of this forest," meant symbolically about mankind. Talking to himself, he relates that he has wounded a boar but lost his quarry and his dogs. Preceded by a fragment of Mélisande's flowing oboe theme and a gently descending figure in the violins, Golaud exclaims that he hears weeping. Seeing Mélisande draped over a fountain, Golaud asks who she is and why she is crying. In her first line, Mélisande cries out for him not to touch her, again, quite metaphorically. As she looks up from the water, Golaud sees that she is beautiful, and says so.

Golaud's curiosity has been roused, and he asks Mélisande if anyone has hurt her. Oh, yes, cries out Mélisande, standing for the lost, injured waif in all of us. Who has hurt her? he inquires. "All of them," she answers, over menacing chords played by the strings and horns. Over a beautiful, soothing melody in the strings, Golaud tells Mélisande not to cry, while she cries that she is lost and was not born here. And where were you born? Golaud asks. "Far, far from here," replies this perpetual outsider.

A tiny horn call sounds as something glimmering in the fountain catches Golaud's eye. It is "the crown he gave me, it fell in while I was weeping." The usually inquisitive Golaud offers to fish it out without asking who "he" is, but Mélisande tells him not to, to an agitated accompaniment in the strings and winds. As he grumbles that the crown would be easy to recover, Mélisande asks Golaud who he is; over a broad and calm accompaniment of horns and bassoons, Golaud identifies himself. With Mélisande's theme sounding sweetly in the winds, she notices his graying hair and beard; already powerfully attracted to her, Golaud asks whether she ever closes her eyes, to a radiant melody that is Mélisande's motif, now revealed in its full beauty. After explaining how he got lost, Golaud asks Mélisande how old she is; evidently as uncomfortable with concrete information as Golaud is desirous of it, she replies over a pulsing figure played by the flutes that she is getting cold. He tells her to come with him; she says no, but to a suave melody in the strings, Golaud says she cannot stay alone in the forest all night. "Where are you going?" Mélisande asks. Lest the audience miss the point that we are all wanderers in this crazy world, Maeterlinck has Golaud reply: "I don't know. I'm lost, too."

As silly as some of the lines may be, Debussy's music carries them easily. Golaud particularly is underplayed, though hardly undercharacterized. His bemused, almost good-humored delivery of the last line in the scene is that of a worldly man who has been lost in the forest before and who feels no panic. In Golaud, moreover, one finds the single recognizable and believable character in this drama of symbolic personages, actions, events, and objects. His actions are those of a real man; as many critics have pointed out, he is the only character in *Pelléas* whose motivations are credible and familiar. Even at his worst, Golaud, like so many people, torments himself as much as Pelléas and Mélisande; he is subject to the same impulses and compulsions everyone experiences. He is sympathetically drawn by Maeterlinck, with his humanity magnified by Debussy's music, and therefore impossible to hate.

The opening scene is tied to the next with an orchestral interlude in which the motif associated with Golaud is heard in the horns over murmuring in the strings. This interlude leads to a marchlike section that bears some resemblance to a far longer passage in act 1 of Wagner's last opera, *Parsifal,* providing perhaps the single, not terribly conspicuous instance of Wagnerian influence in *Pelléas.* In these interludes, Debussy comments on the action, though generally, as with this first one, in an elliptical, un-Wagnerian way. Most of the interludes were shorter or nonexistent in the composer's original conception. They were added and expanded because the Opéra-Comique's stage crew needed more time to change the sets.

The second scene advances the plot considerably. As it opens, Geneviève, the mother of Golaud and Pelléas, is reading a letter from Golaud to old King Arkël (the text never makes clear whether he is her father or father-in-law), who is nearly blind. To a minimal, recitative-like accompaniment, she reads that Golaud has found and married Mélisande, about whom, after six months, he knows "no more about than on the day we met." Fearing Arkël's anger, Golaud asks his half-brother to prepare his return. A lamp in the castle tower will be a sign to Golaud's ship that Arkël has agreed to welcome him home with Mélisande; no lamp means Pelléas has failed and Golaud will sail on. To solemn music led by the brass section that identifies the character throughout the opera, Arkël puts aside his disappointment with Golaud and says he never challenged fate and that "nothing ever occurs uselessly." The grave, oracular tone of Debussy's music, more than the text, suggests that Arkël has learned his fatalism the hard way.

Accompanied by a wavering theme stated by the flutes that captures his passive nature perfectly, Pelléas enters, weeping. Over plaintive chords in the oboes and strings, he tells Geneviève and Arkël that he wants to leave to visit a dying friend, but his grandfather persuades him to remain to wait for Golaud and to be with his own father, who is also ill. The scene ends as the linking interlude begins on a melody sung by

Arkël, here given to a solo violin; the music builds to a big climax for strings alone, with Golaud's theme sung out forcefully by the cellos.

The final scene of the first act, heavily laden with symbolic imagery, begins with a dialogue between Geneviève and Mélisande, whose theme is sung over a rocking figure for the strings by a solo oboe, the plangent tone of which Debussy often associates with her character. Mélisande comments on the darkness of the gardens and forests of the castle. Geneviève (who disappears from the drama without explanation after this scene) agrees but says one gets used to it; she says also that light comes from the direction of the sea, as the strings stab upward as though struggling toward the light. The music builds in animation; Pelléas appears. Commenting also on the brightness on the seaside, he says the ship that brought Mélisande is sailing off and that it may have a rough passage. The strange, haunting cry of the mariners (*Hisse, hoë*—heave, ho) is heard in the distance. After more comments on the falling darkness, to music of sublime beauty and mystery, Pelléas tells Mélisande that he might be leaving the next day. Why? she asks, in the first expression of their attraction, as the music fades down to a quiet close in the flutes, horns, and strings.

Flutes and clarinets state an elegant variant of the Pelléas theme to open act 2. Pelléas has brought Mélisande to a fountain on the grounds of the castle. Rippling figuration in the winds and strings suggests the movement of its waters, which, Pelléas tells Mélisande, were once believed to heal blindness. She leans over the edge, peering eagerly into the water, trying to reach it. A worried Pelléas warns her to be careful, but her hair unravels into the well instead. The water has multiple meanings, here including sex and death. They talk of Golaud, and Mélisande begins to play with the ring he gave her, which, inevitably, falls into the well to a long, dainty *glissando*—a slide of notes—on the harp. Mélisande begins to worry about the ring, tossed into the well with subconscious intent. Debussy's reticence here is remarkable: her words are quickly uttered to the lightest accompaniment imaginable, tiny, delicate, breathless murmurings for the winds and strings. Pelléas tells Mélisande not to worry, that they may find it again, or she can get another. Mélisande, who knows better, wonders what they will tell Golaud about it, to which Pelléas replies, unaccompanied by any instruments but stoutly sung, "The truth!"

This is not, of course, what she does. In the second scene of act 2, set in a room in the castle, the music and drama intensify considerably. The scene's tone is set by a long musical interlude of ever-darkening instrumental color and stronger rhythmic profile. As the scene opens, an injured Golaud describes to Mélisande the strange accident that befell him in the forest at noon, by no coincidence at all the moment she dropped his ring into the well. "I thought my heart was torn in two," he says. Debussy's insistent use of the deep-toned cellos and contrabasses seems to demonstrate the depth and seriousness of Golaud's character. Mélisande offers to bring him water and fix his pillow, but he declines.

Mélisande begins to weep. When Golaud asks why, she tells him that she is ill and unhappy. With a convincing mix of genuine concern and aggression, Golaud presses for further explanation: Has someone offended you? he asks. Is it the king, or his mother, or perhaps Pelléas? No, she answers, it is something stronger than herself. Do you want to leave me? Golaud asks. No, Mélisande replies, but I would like to leave this place with you. Golaud, always looking for material explanations, asks again if Pelléas is snubbing her. He is "rather odd," Golaud tells her, but he'll get over it. He then tells Mélisande, with his concrete, conventional, worldly common sense, that he understands how old, cold, and gloomy the castle is, but that "we can brighten it up...besides, joy is not to be expected every day."

Suddenly, Golaud notices that Mélisande's ring is missing. Abruptly changing from warmly solicitous to menacing, he insists she explain what happened to it. Frightened, she lies to him again, saying she dropped it in a cave by the sea, where she went to find shells for Golaud's son Yniold. Instantly carried away with concern about the ring, he insists she go to find it immediately and take Pelléas with her, throwing them together again inadvertently and bearing out Mélisande's worry in the previous scene about how he would react to the ring's loss. The audience learns here that Golaud is, despite his outward calm, anxious, controlling, materialistic, and a seeker of plain explanations in the face of fundamental mysteries. These qualities only makes him more real and impossible to view as a conventional villain, although he does play the heavy in this tragedy.

From a musical standpoint, the scene is one of the opera's strongest, allowing Debussy room to show power and nimbleness as well as sensitivity. He anticipates Golaud's gruff behavior with the rough passage for strings and horns that opens the scene, and Golaud's short monologue is similarly strongly characterized, though it correctly shows more pain. Again, Mélisande is characterized by soft, high sounds in the winds and strings, and her too-hasty reply when Golaud asks if Pelléas is being unkind shows her true feelings. Golaud's sad description of the chilly, dark castle is set to long, sighing chords in the strings, later joined by the winds. When he reaches for ecstasy in thinking of the summer to come, the full orchestra is there to support him. And nothing could be finer than the change in tone from the moment Golaud sees that his ring is missing from Mélisande's finger, which occurs in real time. Golaud's harrying questions and Mélisande's fluttery, panicked replies receive musical characterizations that are spare, tough, and close to perfect.

The eerie interlude that describes the pointless nighttime excursion of Pelléas and Mélisande to the seaside cave is built of shimmering, trilling strings backed by the icy sound of a cymbal. The doomed pair move carefully on their errand in the near darkness, but Pelléas now joins Mélisande in her deceits by telling her that she must be able to describe the cave to Golaud in case he asks about it. The moonlight breaks through the clouds, to the rapturous notice of the lovers, but their pleasure is tainted by the sight of three old beggars asleep in the cave. Pelléas explains that there is a famine in the land.

Debussy's course in this scene was clear, with low, anxious music dominating the opening sequence, allowing for the big climax as the clouds part to reveal the moon—a moment as glorious as could be expected, though the composer does not linger over it. The music darkens again as Mélisande spots the beggars, and the scene ends, again in mystery and beauty.

The opening scene of act 3 (tracks 2, 3, and 4 on the accompanying CD), set at night at one of the towers of the castle, opens in a magical atmosphere. The tone is set by flutes and two harps. At 0:18 the harp breaks off, while the flutes, accompanied by oboes, state the down-ward-moving theme, gently oscillating between major and minor, that dominates the opening portion of the scene. The glittering opening passage returns (0:31), then the oscillating figure, picked up by bassoons and harps. As the curtain rises, Mélisande stands in the window of the tower, brushing her long hair. She sings a brief ballad (1:00), "Mes longs cheveux" ("My long hair") of timeless beauty reminiscent of the songs of the medieval troubadours: its archaic tone summons eternities of desire. As he often does at crucial moments, Debussy silences the orchestra, letting the slender vocal line carry the full burden of emotion. As Mélisande's song ends, the sweeping figure, musically descriptive of her hair as well as her repetitive combing motion, is heard (2:00) in the lower strings.

An excited flurry in the strings and winds announces Pelléas (2:07). "What are you doing there in the window, singing like a bird who is not from here?" he asks (2:15), "Setting my hair for the night," Mélisande replies. A melody soars, then falls in the strings at 2:26 as Pelléas asks if it is her hair that shines like light against the wall. As the oscillating figure passes from instrument to instrument, Mélisande sings that she has opened the window because it is hot inside the tower (2:37), as Pelléas agrees, noting that he has never seen so many stars (2:53). As the flutes, followed by a small group of the violins, play an excited variant of the oscillating theme, he implores her to lean out the window a little "so [he] can see her hair all undone" (3:13). Mélisande protests that she "looks frightful like this" (3:19). To a surging phrase in the strings at 3:25, Pelléas tells her how beautiful she is, then asks her once more to lean out, to come closer. To another of the many falling phrases that dominate the scene, Mélisande says that she "cannot come close to him" (3:39). "I cannot climb higher," he answers (3:49); he then tells her, again, that he is leaving the next day (3:58) and, accompanied by urgent rippling in the violins, that he wants to put her hand to his lips (4:14).

Mélisande knows better, as by now does the audience. "You will not leave tomorrow," she replies, while the bassoons sing the combing motif in slower notes and the lower strings trill excitedly like barely repressed emotions (4:22), and of course, Pelléas immediately replies that he will wait. Mélisande spots a rose down in the garden, which Pelléas promises to look for, but only after she has given him her hand (4:58). She leans farther out the window, fretting that she will fall, as the falling figure sounds first in the flutes and oboes, then the lower woodwinds (5:13). As she leans, Mélisande's long hair tumbles from the tower, signaled at 5:30 by a gentle avalanche in the strings. Pelléas expresses his joy in short, excited phrases (5:34–5:50).

The music slows as Pelléas sings his rapturous tribute to Mélisande's hair (track 3). He will hold it in his hands, his mouth, his arms, and he will wrap it around his neck, he sings, accompanied by the clarinet in a dreamy version of the big melody that was first heard at 2:26, which Debussy uses again and again here to emphasize Pelléas's obsession, as he does with the falling figure that accompanied the fall of Mélisande's hair from the tower (0:12, 0:36, and phrased differently at 0:55). This wonderful seductress languidly protests (0:19), "Leave me, you will make me fall." Wrapping himself in her hair, Pelléas tells Mélisande that he has never seen hair so long and soft; to a phrase of religious solemnity at 1:10, he sings that "he can no longer see the sky" through it. Then, in a passionate solo beginning at 1:15 that is about as close as one can find in *Pelléas* to an aria, he sings that he cannot hold her hair, "which spreads out like the branches of a willow, it is like living birds between my hands. And it loves me . . . more than you."

But Debussy once again makes his score move with the text. Once Pelléas has sung his ecstatic lines, the drama flows on, as Mélisande unconvincingly protests (1:40). Pelléas tells her he will hold her prisoner all night, to which she breathes his name passionately (2:05). To the now dreamlike accompaniment of the big, passionate melody from earlier, he begins to tie her hair to the branches of a willow (2:12). As Pelléas kisses Mélisande's hair, he asks if she can hear the kisses traveling to her, the orchestra surging once more, though not loudly, to this powerful erotic image (2:49).

The texture suddenly lightens and the music speeds up as, at 3:15, the violins play a shuddering, rhythmically altered version of the sensuous melody. Mélisande cries out that he is hurting her, then asks what the fluttering sound was; Pélleas answers that it was the doves he startled. They—symbolic, presumably, of lost innocence—will not come back in the dark, she laments (3:40). The music darkens, with horns, bassoons, and tympani asserting themselves as Mélisande hears approaching footsteps. She fears that it may be Golaud, who indeed enters as Pelléas fumbles to untie her hair (4:01). His entrance (track 4) is accompanied by gruff chords in the strings. "What are you doing here?" he asks his brother, who of course cannot reply. "You are children," he grumbles (0:10), predictably and perhaps a bit tiresomely warning Mélisande not to lean out the window, that it's late (0:32), and then, again, that they are children, such children . . . such children (0:39, 0:41, and 0:43). He and Pelléas leave.

The slow orchestral interlude that follows seems to paint the suspicion that has sprouted in Golaud's mind, but it does so without overstatement. Beginning with Golaud's motif in the strings (1:00), it passes uneasily to the oboes. At 1:29 Mélisande's theme appears in the violins, then the flutes (1:46), and finally returns to the oboe, its primary instrument, at 2:10. At 2:15, Pelléas's wavering theme can be heard below it in the violas and then, at 2:30, played by the English horn, clarinets, and bassoons. At 3:10 there is a rumble from the tympani, accompanied by somber chords from the clarinets, bassoons, and horns, as the trumpet, strikingly used against type by Debussy as a symbol of darkness, sings out a bleak five-note phrase.

For the prurient—presumably everyone—subsequent events will make clear that Pelléas and Mélisande never consummate their love. The lines in which they sing that they "can never reach" each other already suggest this, but the erotic power of their attraction seems greater for that. Golaud's reaction at finding them entangled illustrates the nature of their relationship: their "childish" game is clearly sexual, yet he also correctly sees both as utterly unworldly. Whether or not they have slept together, they act like lovers, making Golaud's doubts as to their innocence unavoidable.

The next scene, short but intense, takes place in the vaults beneath the castle, where Golaud has led Pelléas. Without openly threatening his younger half-brother, Golaud, asks if he does not smell the scent of death there and guides him to the edge of a chasm. Crying out that he is stifling, Pelléas begs to leave. As one would expect, Debussy uses the low-toned instruments to paint a terrifying picture of the darkness, even holding these to the bottoms of their ranges, in a standard but effective compositional technique in which visual darkness is equated with low musical tones.

Pelléas and Golaud mount the stairs to one of the castle terraces. It is now daylight, represented by the glory of the full orchestra, in an interlude that, in its brightening orchestral colors (including flutes, harps, trumpets, cymbals, and violins) and sharp rhythmic profile, contrasts in the strongest way possible with the gloom of the previous scene; it also clearly anticipates the first movement of *La mer,* which paints a similar picture of the sun rising over the ocean. Pelléas sings with gratitude of the daylight, the sun, the gardens and their beauty; he notices that it is noon, even though it didn't seem that he and Golaud were in the vault for quite so long—it's good to remember that the action in *Pelléas* is symbolic and hardly literal.

Pelléas spots Mélisande standing in the shade of the tower; Golaud takes the opportunity to say blandly that he "heard what was going on and what was said last night." He knows it was "a childish game, but it mustn't happen again." He then notes with a bit more edge that "it's not the first time I've noticed that there might be something between you," and that from now on Pelléas should avoid Mélisande, but "not too pointedly."

Long, complex, painful to watch, and difficult to bring off in performance, the final scene of act 3 begins with a short interlude in which burbling figures in the winds alternate with somber chords in the strings and brass; as it ends, the oboe sings a new, lilting melody used mostly in the presence of Golaud's son Yniold. This is the moment when Golaud's suspicions about Mélisande and Pelléas take on flesh, as he presses his boy brutally for information about the couple. Indeed, Golaud's worst traits are on display, as he expresses jealousy at Mélisande for the time Yniold spends with her and nags the boy not to put his fingers in his mouth.

But his self-torturing suspicion and willingness to employ his child as an unwitting informer and spy are far worse. He begins questioning Yniold calmly about whether "Mommy [Mélisande is the child's stepmother] and Uncle Pelléas" spend much time together, to which he receives the troubling answer "Yes, always when you aren't there."

Golaud asks whether they argue, and what about; Yniold gives the baffling reply "The door." Yniold tells Golaud further that they talk a great deal about him (Yniold) and, more comfortingly, that he is "always beside them," hinting again at their physical chastity. Golaud is now convinced of their guilt; nothing can deflect him from his jealous trajectory. He asks if they have kissed, to which Yniold tells him yes, once, when it was raining. Beside himself, Golaud tells the little boy to climb onto his shoulders and look into Mélisande's window. Pelléas is with her, though they are not touching, moving, or even talking. What are they doing, then? "Looking at the light." Golaud wants Yniold to continue spying, but the terrified child threatens to scream, and his infuriated father finally allows him to run off.

With its feeling of Golaud going out of control, behaving abusively toward his young son, the scene is genuinely painful to watch. Debussy builds the tension effectively, using Yniold's little tune with increasing vehemence as the scene progresses and pushing the dialogue with coiled rhythms that never let up. The last couple of minutes are carried on a constant flow of triplets, a common device of three notes played in the space of two, creating a throbbing pulse. Again, the unsentimental portrait of Golaud in the text and the music are all too believable. Jealousy is one of the common themes of opera; with Golaud's jealousy out in the open, comparisons with Otello's expression of the emotion in Verdi's masterpiece are inevitable, and perhaps unflattering to *Pelléas*. But *Otello* is the greatest study of jealousy in opera, and quite possibly the greatest in Western art; here, Debussy's portrayal of Golaud's self-destructive jealousy remains pitched, like the rest of *Pelléas*, relatively low. The portrait of a man making everyone—but himself, above all—miserable is sadly convincing, from both dramatic and musical standpoints.

Act 4 represents the climax of external action in this inward drama. After a brief orchestral prelude that is agitated but fluid, Pelléas and Mélisande meet in a hall of the castle. Saying he that he must speak to her that night, he relates that his father, who had been gravely ill, is recovering; that he had recognized Pelléas, but noticed that his son "had the serious, friendly air of one who hasn't long to live." He says, again, that he is leaving, and that Mélisande will never see him again after this last rendezvous, which they set at the Blind Man's Well. Mélisande replies that she "shall always see" him. Hearing people approach, Pelléas leaves. The scurrying winds and strings vividly portray the furtiveness of a relationship that, whether consummated or not, is now absolutely illicit.

The speed of the music moderates as Arkël enters the hall. In a long monologue, he tells Mélisande of the recovery of Pelléas's father, and of his own hopes that "a little joy and sunlight will at last come into the house again." Arkël then tells her how sad it made him to see her youth and beauty isolated in the gloomy castle "under the shadow of death." Musing on the nature of life, the old king sings that he has "gained a kind of faith in the fidelity of events" and that the lovely Mélisande will be the one to open a beautiful new era in Allemonde, Debussy building the music here to one of the few big climaxes in the score, a visionary moment that matches Arkël's fervor. Then, in one of the opera's most insightful passages, Arkël asks Mélisande to allow him to kiss her, since even "old men need to put their lips now and then to a woman's brow or a child's cheek, to go on believing in the freshness of life and to drive away for a moment the threat of death." Arkël, who is nearly blind, still sees well enough for Mélisande's beauty to be obvious to him; in his age, infirmity, and hard-won wisdom, the old king still cannot resist her. The quiet music that accompanies these words expresses an infinity of sensual longing.

Golaud, now a dangerous man, enters agitatedly, to grumbling in the lower strings. Brusquely he tells Mélisande and Arkël that Pelléas is to leave that evening. Mélisande notices blood on his forehead, but Golaud repulses with disgust her offer to wipe it away. He asks Mélisande for his sword, which she brings. In a long, excited monologue, he asks Mélisande why she is trembling, that he is not going to kill her, although that is clearly on his mind. Looking into her eyes, he says, "Look into those great eyes . . . one would think they are proud of their riches." Arkël replies that they contain nothing but great innocence, the wrong thing to say to his grandson, who continues his rant with greater rage and less coherence. In a passage virtually parallel to one in *Otello,* Golaud grabs Mélisande's hand, which he calls "too hot . . . your flesh disgusts me!" Mad with rage, he grabs her by the hair ("useful for something at last"), pulls her to her knees, then back and forth, calling out the name of Absalom, a biblical prince who was trapped by his long hair, and he throws his wife to the ground (as Otello does Desdemona), laughing madly. Just before Arkël rebukes him, Golaud cries out that he is "already laughing like an old man." Nearing its peak of violence, the music is filled with sharp gestures and thematic fragments that mirror Golaud's disturbance and physicality, with swooping, shuddering runs in the violins, and the horns taking on the coloristic burden, barking and chattering fearfully.

Suddenly calm, Golaud says tells his wife to "do what you like . . . I don't play the spy," a fine insight of Maeterlinck's, as that is precisely what he recently did. Ominously, Golaud mutters that he will "wait on chance . . . and then . . . just because it's customary." There is no need for him to spell out what is "customary," for the audience understands that he is now bent on avenging himself on Pelléas and Mélisande. After Golaud leaves, Arkël asks Mélisande what is wrong with him; in the understatement that brought derisive laughter in the opera's first performances, Mélisande replies, " . . . he doesn't love me anymore . . . I'm unhappy," to which Arkël, accompanied by horns, trombones, and tuba, replies with prophetic solemnity: "If I were God, I should have pity on the hearts of men."

The heavy brass and heavier atmosphere remain in place for the interlude that follows, the longest and most clearly expressive of all. Based entirely on the theme associated with Golaud, its tone of sorrow is unmistakable; it is interesting that Debussy chose to emphasize at this crucial moment that the tragedy is that of the real man, Golaud, as much, and perhaps more, than that of the insubstantial title characters.

One scene, highly symbolic in nature, intervenes before the playing out of Pelléas's tragedy. Yniold has lost his ball behind a boulder while playing by the Blind Man's Well outside the castle. He laments that his arm is too short to reach behind and that he is too small to lift the stone. Yniold's music here has a rapid, almost playful quality, expressing more the weightless energy of youth than frustration. Suddenly he hears the bleating of sheep. He worries that they are "frightened of the dark . . . huddling together." The shepherd is driving them in an unaccustomed direction, and they are confused and frightened. When Yniold asks the shepherd why they have suddenly quieted, he is told that "this isn't the way to the sheepfold." Switching again to a heavy-handed symbolism, Maeterlinck makes it clear that the sheep have gone to the slaughterhouse instead, and—surprise!—that they stand for Pelléas and Mélisande, who are also about to meet their doom.

The final scene of the act opens as Yniold leaves, and Pelléas appears for his final meeting with Mélisande. Soliloquizing for a moment that it is for them the last night, he expresses the conflicting emotions that grip him, concluding that he "must tell her the things I haven't said." Mélisande appears, and, in another of those heart-stopping moments when Debussy allows the characters' highest emotions to speak without a note from the orchestra, the lovers greet each other. After a discussion of darkness and light, the words to which clearly rely on the big duet in act 2 of *Tristan,* Pelléas quietly declares his love to Mélisande, who replies in kind; the orchestra remains silent. In a long passage that builds slowly in intensity over the remainder of the scene, Pelléas rhapsodizes at great length, asking Mélisande whether she is not lying just to make him smile. She answers: "No, I never lie; only to your brother." In keeping with Mélisande's quietness, most of the musical excitement belongs to Pelléas, whereas her replies are shorter and more subdued.

The lovers (not the audience, however) hear the bolts being drawn shut on the castle doors, and they are locked out, literally as well as metaphorically; abandoning all ties with the world, they embrace each other and their isolation. There is a rustling in the leaves; it is Golaud, of course, who strikes his brother down without a word. Mélisande flees, crying out that she is a coward. And the act ends in one of the score's handful of violent musical gestures.

The musicologist and critic Joseph Kerman comments sharply about the final scene of act 4 in his landmark 1956 study *Opera as Drama,* "It is the rare opera in which the love music is the least effective" (190). Kerman's view may be strongly put, but in it he is not alone. Listeners looking for a love duet that resembles those of *Otello, Tristan,* or almost any opera one might mention are bound for disappointment. This duet is as restrained in its musical language as the rest of the opera, with only Pelléas showing any ardency, and Mélisande responding with her typical taciturnity. The music accelerates when it should, and Debussy instructs the orchestra to play "with transport" as the lovers' excitement (or at least Pelléas's excitement) builds, and the instrumental colors darken correctly and predictably as Golaud stalks them. But of the hot emotion that typically grabs listeners—the oxygen for opera's fire—there is little to be found. Debussy's music is filled with ecstasy, but not of the operatic type. He screened and filtered rudimentary emotions like those expressed in a typical operatic love duet from nearly all of his music, including this scene.

The fifth and last act takes place in a single long, sorrowful scene. Mélisande, whom Golaud injured slightly after killing Pelléas, is inexplicably dying from her wound. She has also given birth to her and Golaud's daughter; there is no question that anyone but he is the father. In the room with her are a physician, Arkël, and Golaud, now wracked with guilt and self-loathing. The scene opens with a sad rising and falling theme associated with Mélisande; as the curtain rises, the doctor says her wound is too small to kill even a bird. Arkël replies that her slow breathing is a bad sign. As his theme sounds uneasily in the horns, Golaud laments that he has killed without reason, that Pelléas and Mélisande had only "kissed like little children . . . they were brother and sister . . . I did it despite myself."

Mélisande wakes, asking for the window to be opened, another ominous sign symbolically, for it is through the window through that her spirit will soon depart. Surprisingly, she says that she has never felt better, but that "it seems as though I knew something." When Arkël asks what she means, Mélisande replies, typically, "I don't know what I'm saying. I don't know what I know. I can't say what I want to say anymore," a verbal parallel with the theme that opened the act, rising weakly before falling back upon itself.

Arkël tells Mélisande that Golaud is in the room, but that she should not be afraid, which, already letting go of life and purged of emotion, she is not. As he approaches her bed, Mélisande tells Golaud that he looks older and thinner. Golaud asks the others to leave the room so he may speak to his wife alone, saying, "don't refuse me this . . . I'm wretchedly unhappy." When they have left, he asks Mélisande if she can forgive him, to which she replies, "Yes . . . what must I forgive you for?" Golaud embarks on a long, agonized litany of the harm he has done her, saying that everything is his fault and that he loved her so very much. As the music builds to a surprisingly fierce climax, Golaud, unable to let go of his need for hard information, says he must know "the truth. Did you love Pelléas?" "Why, yes," she answers quietly and simply, "where is he?"

Golaud has not finished his inquest. "Don't you understand? . . . I'm asking if your love for him was a forbidden love. Were . . . the pair of you guilty?" With real insight, Maeterlinck has Golaud provide the answer he perversely desires: "Tell me, yes, yes, yes." Using the strings in low notes a sharp rhythm, Debussy seems to have grasped the author's intentions clearly, beautifully heightening the expressiveness of Golaud's words and the emotion that lies beneath them. Mélisande replies that she and Pelléas were not guilty. Still wracked with jealousy, Golaud begs Mélisande for the truth he wants to hear, saying that she mustn't lie on the point of death. Surprised to hear that she is dying, Mélisande fades out of consciousness murmuring, "The truth . . . the truth . . ." as Golaud mourns bitterly that "she's already too far gone . . . I shall never know! I shall die in blindness."

Arkël and the doctor reenter the room. The old king and Mélisande briefly talk about the fading light and the onset of winter; he then asks if she wants to see her newborn daughter. Confused and failing, Mélisande says, "I can't lift my arms to take her," as Arkël brings the infant over for her to see. "She doesn't smile. She is very small. She's going to cry. I feel sorry for her," Mélisande murmurs, her last words perhaps the weightiest she utters. Sensing Mélisande's imminent death, the serving women of the castle enter the room, silently lining the rear wall and angering Golaud, who expresses himself to the sharp sound of plucked string instruments. Watching Mélisande closely, Arkël observes that her eyes are filled with tears; Golaud rages for the others to leave him alone with her. No, his grandfather commands, "don't speak to her anymore. You don't know what the soul is." Once more, Golaud sobs that it wasn't his fault.

As the music fades to near silence, the servants fall to their knees; Mélisande is gone. To a very beautiful accompaniment high in the strings, Arkël comments that "the human soul is a very silent thing."

As Golaud sobs, the old king comforts his grandson, saying: "It's terrible, but it wasn't your fault. She was such a quiet little creature, so timid and so silent. She was a poor little mysterious being like all of us." Then, speaking of the baby, he says, "It's the poor little thing's turn." For the exquisite orchestral postlude that brings this quietest of operas to its quiet close, Debussy employs a tiny, falling melodic interval in a miniscule rhythm; it is one he would employ again in a slightly different form in the 1904 song *Auprès de cette grotte sombre* and in *Des pas sur la neige* from Book I of the *Préludes*, in both, as here, expressing isolation, desolation, and infinite regret.

Pour le Piano II: *Masterpieces of the Middle Years*

ebussy composed some of the most significant monuments of
the keyboard literature between 1901, when he completed *Pour
le piano,* and the 1910 publication of the first set of preludes. In
this decade Debussy achieved a style that changed the sound of piano
music once and for all, comparable to the way in which he also discovered new orchestral colors, finding in the bulky, beloved contraption of
wood and metal many tone colors barely hinted at by even his greatest
predecessors. He would later refine—and refine considerably—what
he mined from the instrument, but in a sense he never surpassed what
he achieved during this period.

Debussy composed only two works for two pianos, but the lovely
Lindaraja, composed in 1901, is utterly neglected; the very late masterwork *En blanc et noir* is perhaps the greatest of all compositions for this
awkward combination. Unlike its successor, *Lindaraja* is easy to underrate. The short work is in the form of a habanera, the Spanish dance
that fascinated French composers most; the best known is that from
Act I of Bizet's *Carmen,* to which the heroine sings the words *"L'amour
est un oiseau rebelle"* with the characteristic snapping accompaniment
(long–short–long–long). Debussy himself would use the habanera
rhythm in the middle movement of *Ibéria,* the prelude *La Puerta del
Vino,* and, most notably, only two years later, *Soirée dans Grenade,* for
which *Lindaraja* seems a study. Charming, hypnotic, and very beautiful, *Lindaraja* would be a sure crowd-pleaser and eminently deserves
rehabilitation.

Estampes (the word means "engravings," though perhaps the second
dictionary definition, "prints," is more accurate in this instance) is

one of the revolutionary works in Debussy's output and in the keyboard literature, which it divides into what came before and after. In fact, Western "classical" music has not been the same since the 1903 composition of these three short pieces. It is not difficult to trace the evolution of Debussy's piano style toward *Estampes* in the works that precede it, such as, for example, in the tone painting of *Clair de lune* or in the ironic gravity of the sarabande in *Pour le piano.* But the changes Debussy devised in the three *Estampes* are profound: gone are the suites modeled on baroque forms; each work stands on its own and can be played individually, with no loss of context or integrity.

The most important changes Debussy achieved in the *Estampes* are the new dominance of pictorialism and an absolute alteration in the kind of sounds listeners expect a piano to make. These three pieces find their roots in other cultures, notably East Asian and Spanish music, and in the nursery songs of France; they have a powerful visual component, as well. In the second *Estampe, Soirée dans Grenade,* Debussy builds a bold structure of utter originality based on the perception of a number of sounds and sights—all imagined by the composer—rather than the demands of a preexisting musical form. This is music that describes how people perceive the world. The piano sounds Debussy creates in these three extraordinary pieces represent perhaps their most daring aspect, a revolution as great as that wrought by his predecessor and idol Chopin. From the faraway, chiming beauties of *Pagodes* to the smoky nocturne that is *Soirée dans Grenade,* to the images of sunlight glinting after a rain in *Jardins sous la pluie,* Debussy uncovered in this percussion instrument coloristic capabilities never before imagined.

The quiet, droning chords that open the tone poem *Pagodes* mark the extent of Debussy's revolution. For with these atmospheric chords, Debussy sets the stage for what is to follow. In this great work, he also sums up of the effects of the Asian music he heard performed at the 1889 Exposition Universelle by Javanese *gamelan* orchestras. These orchestras include strings, woodwinds, and a wide range of percussion instruments, including gongs, chimes, and marimbas, creating soft, buzzing tone colors, quite unlike those of their Western counterparts; it is easy to hear them in the fine balance of delicacy and power in Debussy's piano writing. After these chords, which seem to float rather than move in any direction, a melody enters, similarly hovering in character. Debussy achieves its peculiar motionlessness by employing a five-note scale, common in the music of Southeast Asia. This scale lacks the major and minor inflections on which Western ears rely for hints about the music's emotional content, with major often suggesting brighter feelings and the minor keys offering almost certain clues of struggle and sorrow.

Soon, Debussy introduces a fervent, winding melodic strand, narrow in range and buried inside the middle of the keyboard. Melodic cells, rather than themes, appear and depart, some displaying greater activity, others more stilly floating in gentle succession, subject only to decoration, never dissected or placed into conflict as in a sonata development. One melody rises majestically in volume above the rest, but in no sense is it the winner in some kind of thematic battle; it functions as merely another character in a grand procession of Asian-inspired themes. Debussy might almost have changed the order of the many melodic cells without altering the character of *Pagodes,* yet the piece is neither light nor loose. The long and very beautiful passage that ends *Pagodes* brings back the winding melody heard early in the work, this time amid lavish figuration. The emotions evoked by this great work are profound but difficult to name—they have something to do with the childlike wonder and longing felt for remote places, and their sights, sounds, scents, and names. The revolutionary floating harmonies and sonorities of *Pagodes* capture this sensation with remarkable power.

Every book about Debussy is duty bound to report that his time in Spain was limited to an afternoon in the Basque city of San Sebastián, near the French border. This information is important because Debussy composed so much "Spanish" music and because his grasp of the Spanish popular idiom is so powerful. This skill is nowhere more starkly evident than in *Soirée dans Grenade* (Evening in Granada; track 5 on the CD), the stunning work that is the centerpiece of *Estampes.* Held together by the tense rhythm of the habanera, *Soirée dans Grenade* is more than an evocation of the power and exoticism of Spanish music. Like its companions in *Estampes,* it stands as one of Debussy's astounding ventures into the musical expression of perception and, as a daring experiment in the crosscutting of themes, foreshadows later achievements in cinema.

This may sound like a lot to be packed into a six-page score that takes the legendary Russian pianist Sviatoslav Richter just five and a half minutes to play, but it's all in there.

Soirée dans Grenade opens with the tense and hypnotic long–short–long–long rhythm of the *habanera,* quietly setting the atmosphere. The rhythm runs through the piece, unifying its many disjunctions. At 0:14, a sinuous and passionate melody enters underneath, running until 0:40. Based on the *cante jondo* (deep song) of the southern province of Andalusia, it is rich with eroticism, despair, and ululating Moorish accents; Debussy would use it as a model for the more violent *La Puerta del Vino* from Book II of the *Préludes* and for the first movement of the Sonata for Cello and Piano. A new theme cuts in almost abruptly at 0:42, chords that wonderfully mimic the strumming of a guitar. Debussy's musical ancestor Chopin produces similar effects in several of his mazurkas, the Polish folk dance he elevated to high art; Debussy used the full orchestra to imitate the guitar, though to very different effect, in the final section of the orchestral tone poem *Ibéria.*

A new, rising, vocally styled theme appears at 0:52, followed again by the strumming figure at 1:09 and a falling phrase that sounds like the wailing of a singer (1:16). At 1:26, a new rhythmic phrase, expressing a more exalted emotion, appears, into which Debussy winds the first melody (beginning at 1:32), which plays itself out in sinking phrases over a strict habanera rhythm. The rising phrase (first heard at 0:52) returns, clothed in more bitter harmony (2:11). The long passage that is the emotional heart of the work begins at 2:29, a passionate new melody in the right hand. Debussy interweaves major and minor tonalities densely throughout (at 2:38, 2:42, and 2:45, for example), as the idealized singer of the *cante jondo* expresses joy and pain that are inseparable—and perhaps even joy *in* suffering. But in keeping with the smoldering atmosphere of *Soirée dans Grenade,* the volume remains low. A comparable passage at the heart of Chopin's wonderful Mazurka in C-sharp minor, op. 30, no. 4, may have provided Debussy with his inspiration here.

After the melodic roulades of this song of passion wind down, the strumming figure recurs (3:29), followed by an elaborate passage in which the long opening melody against the habanera rhythm, here (3:39

and on) filled out in ecstatic harmony. Then, after that rhythm is taken down to its most basic form deep in the bass (3:58), comes the first of the protocinematic cuts, as a completely new thematic element, a quick jingling over a scurrying accompaniment, interrupts (4:02), perhaps representing the clicking of castanets or the harnesses of bells worn by the mules that carry passengers and merchandise in southern Spain. This astonishing effect portrays something happening simultaneously with the *cante jondo* but coming from another direction, as the ear might hear two things at once. Another abrupt cut returns to the passionate melody first heard at 2:29, here heard as a fragment, interrupted (4:17) by the jingling phrase. The interrupted song comes back, leading into the long, hypnotic closing section; listen at 4:34 for the opening melody and at 4:53 for the final appearance of the strumming figure, denuded of harmony and heard as though fading away. The habanera quietly holds sway to the very end.

The fine Spanish composer Manuel de Falla, in speech and prose, called *Soirée dans Grenade* the greatest "Spanish" work for piano (Schmitz 85–86). It is also one of Debussy's most gripping, fully imagined compositions, a tremendous study of how a listener might actually experience a performance of an Andalusian *cante jondo*—emotionally as well as aurally—with other sounds passing into and out of hearing.

Jardins sous la pluie (Gardens in the Rain) ends *Estampes* on a brilliant note, and, like its companions, the music is of stunning imaginative depth. A technically demanding work for skilled pianists only, *Jardins sous la pluie* is based on mechanical difficulties examined by Bach in the Inventions and Chopin in the etudes and preludes. The hammering individual notes paint a picture of how human senses perceive a garden shivering beneath a dual assault of rain and wind. While *Jardins sous la pluie* flows quickly, like the toccata that concludes *Pour le piano,* and serves a comparable cathartic role, Debussy's tone painting gives the later work a deeper emotional resonance. The two French nursery songs *Dodo, l'enfant do* and *Nous n'irons pas au bois,* inserted in the middle suggest that it is not just the storm pictured, but children watching, with fascination and perhaps a shiver of terror, from indoors. The entry of the nursery songs is utterly natural, with no sense that extraneous material is being imposed to create a sense of false profundity.

Thunderous octaves in the left hand suggest the approach of a big climax, but, in his typical manner, Debussy forces his listeners to adjust their expectations by breaking the passage off abruptly. Trills suggest the wind, and in tiny notes and glittering arpeggios Debussy reveals with genius the at-first tentative return of the sun and the dancing of the dripping water in its light; the work ends in a brilliant upward run that Debussy would use again in the prelude *Les collines d'Anacapri,* to tell us that the sun is out in glory once again. He may have borrowed this idea from Chopin, who concluded the cheerful Mazurka in D major, op. 33, no. 2, with a similar phrase. Despite its speed and brilliance, *Jardins sous la pluie* is intense and layered.

Two compositions share 1904 as their date of publication. *L'isle joyeuse* (The Joyful Isle) is a high-spirited but sensuous virtuoso piece, inspired by the Rococo painter Antoine Watteau's mythological painting *L'embarquement pour Cythère* and formally modeled on Chopin's Ballade no. 3. This glorious essay in dance rhythm opens unforgettably with a long trill, which leads into a winding figure, then the swaying and trembling rhythm that is unmistakably choreographic. Tension builds steadily, even through moments of lesser release, as the glorious main melody appears over huge arpeggios in the left hand. Playful figuration breaks the tune off, but crashing chords develop into a secondary climax, followed by more urgent, driving incarnations of earlier material as the main theme sings out in all its glory, leading into a brief, triumphant coda.

Masques, on the other hand, has always baffled pianists and audiences alike; as a result, it is rarely performed. A strange, clangorous rhythmic figure dominates the work, communicating tension and, later, grimmer emotions. Even the quieter middle part is restless, and when Debussy brings back the opening, it is clothed in strange harmonies. The pianist Marguerite Long, who studied with the composer, described *Masques* as "a tragedy for piano" (qtd. in Roberts 101); certainly it seems comfortless, even chilling. Rarely even recorded, *Masques* is an important work by one of the greatest composers, awaiting rediscovery and sympathetic rehabilitation.

Following the bold lines laid out in *Estampes,* Debussy composed two sets of piano pieces called *Images,* the first in 1905, the second two years later. *Estampes* is so transcendently great that it would be wrong to call the *Images* an advance, but they do maintain the same artistic level, no mean feat. All three sets for the piano, as well as the *Images* for orchestra, share pictorial and experiential natures, describing through music how people perceive the world, not only through hearing, but visually.

Formally, *Estampes* and the three sets of *Images* comprise three independent pieces that may or may not be played consecutively, or together. *Ibéria,* the second of the orchestral *Images,* is in three movements and has always been performed more than its companion works. In a 1957 recital in London, Arturo Benedetti Michelangeli, the pianist in most of the solo works on the CD that accompanies this book, made a suite of four of the six *Images,* playing them out of sequence but beginning with the slowest, *Et la lune descend sur la temple qui fût,* and ending with the most flowing of the four, *Reflets dans l'eau.* Michelangeli's logic and stunning playing (the performance was recorded) justify his ordering without a hint of trouble. The point here is simply that these works are decidedly independent, not suites like *Pour le piano* or the *bergamasque.* The three separate movements of *La mer,* as well as those that form *Ibéria* (two of which are linked musically), on the other hand, form unified, potent wholes.

Debussy was fascinated by water in its various forms; he learned to portray it in his music with unmatched success. Franz Liszt preceded him in using the resources of the keyboard to describe the element aurally in its rippling and flowing incarnations, but Debussy surpassed Liszt in capturing water in other states. He renders the sound and sight of rain with clarity in *Jardins sous la pluie,* while in *Poissons d'or* (Goldfish) from the second set of *Images,* one can feel the trembling of the water in which the fish move. *Reflets dans l'eau* (Reflections in the Water; track 6), first of the *Images,* shows light refracted on water that is not quite still, moving more rapidly, then slowing again.

It is impossible when listening to *Reflets dans l'eau* to mistake in the opening chord in the bass, above which even chords shimmer gracefully, the look of gently moving water. (Harder to explain is how sound can so clearly suggest sight!) At 0:34, 0:40, and 0:44, rippling notes interrupt the languorous opening page, stirring lazily (1:07) before moving at 1:11 into a steady pattern of faster notes. In the more rapid passagework that follows, one can feel the swifter flow, finally reaching, between 2:29 and 3:20, several radiant climaxes that reveal the splendor of light on moving water. These flashes of ecstasy are, however, also of typical Debussyan brevity: he is creating a picture, not showing off. On the closing page the music slows again, as shimmering individual notes (from 3:56 to the end) unmistakably evoke droplets falling into the pool. Debussy's fascination with light and movement—his recognition that nothing is ever still and his genius at rendering gentle movement in tone—probes at the very nature of perception and reality. *Reflets dans l'eau* is a visionary expression of this truth.

Hommage à Rameau (Homage to Rameau; track 7 on the CD) is Debussy's grandest tribute to his musical ancestor, the composer Jean-Philippe Rameau (1683–1764) and to the glory of the music of his homeland during the baroque era. Rameau, an energetic and multi-faceted composer of genius, produced lively, brightly colored works in many genres, including opera, ballet, sacred music, and suites for the harpsichord. Debussy's piece is in the form of a sarabande, a slow dance much used in instrumental suites of the baroque era, also employed by Debussy as the second movement of *Pour le piano*. With its slow tempo, the sarabande is generally a stately vehicle for profound emotions, as it is in this case, with a melancholy nostalgia predominating here. Although of gripping power, *Hommage à Rameau* eschews a tragic posture; its feelings seem remote and somehow abstract. It is another outstanding example among many of music about music in Debussy's oeuvre.

Before a note of *Hommage à Rameau* is heard, Debussy's indication for tempo and expression says much about the mood of the piece: slow and grave, in the style of a sarabande, but without rigor. The long opening phrase, ripe with triplets (0:05, 0:11–0:12, and 0:16–0:18) that are integral to its character, and a thoughtful pause at its center (0:10) seems to float. The second portion appears (0:20) over a booming note in the bass as stately chords in the left hand support the melody in the right. The opening spins itself out in triplets in the right hand and austere octaves in the left, followed by another long pause. At 0:48 the melody recurs, marked (0:54) by a variation in its rhythm and phrasing; at 1:09, Debussy introduces a new figure, with a broader emotional range and garbed in richer harmony. This new figure builds into a more pressing rhythm (1:35) and a majestic chord sequence in which the melody is embedded. This sequence reaches a climax (2:04), after which the opening phrase brings this section of the work to a quietly sinking close (2:18).

A serious new melody enters quietly at 2:45, in a new rhythm and with a strange, faraway harmony. Note also the melodic figure that floats in gently at 3:14, then repeats in deeper notes at 3:20 and 3:27, as, along with booming octaves in the bass, it forms the background to the magnificent passage that follows, where it moves beneath the restless harmony of big right-hand chords (3:35 and on). Chopin's influence can be detected in the rich keyboard textures and daring harmony. At 4:04 occurs the climax of this central portion, the strange melody first heard at 2:45, here thundered out in heavy chords, interspersed with sweeping arpeggios at 4:08, 4:16, 4:19, and 4:23. The expression here is grand, and the emotion expressed in this section is powerful—but also powerfully enigmatic.

The long, dying fall that is the closing passage of *Hommage à Rameau* begins at 4:29, with the return of the opening melody, reharmonized as though spent, over gentle pulsations in the bass. The recurrence of the theme's second phrase (4:47) briefly suggests a return to strength, but in fact Debussy is unraveling his material in a slow, steady progress toward the end. A long pause at 5:12 precedes the breakup of the opening melody, now in chords decorated by the melodic figure that played a crucial role in moving the middle section to its climax, first in the left hand at 5:21, then in the right at 5:31, 5:37, 5:50, and 6:04. Majestic but elusive, *Hommage à Rameau* fades out on an enormous chord, struck gently in the bass, then the treble.

Mouvement, third and last of the first set of *Images*, is a more slender work, animated by dance rhythms and glittering keyboard figuration rather than melody, intended by Debussy to be in a lighter tone. What emerges as a big tune is nothing more than a series of plain chords, moving downward, scalewise; the middle section features figuration that scampers over the keyboard, presenting a contrast in pianistic texture but not in speed; the opening returns and the work dies out in a grotesque passage, anticipating Stravinsky, where the hands move apart. Generally, the percussive rhythms of *Mouvement* look ahead to the work of Debussy's friend Stravinsky, particularly, as the biographer Edward Lockspeiser has pointed out, the younger composer's ballet *Petrushka* of 1911 (150).

By the time Debussy wrote the second series of *Images,* the growing complexity of his technique demanded that this music for a pair of hands be written out on three lines instead of the normal two. There is nothing straightforward about the first set, but in this trio, the music has turned into "something rich and strange." The first piece, *Cloches à travers les feuilles* (literally "bells across the leaves," a free translation for clarity being "Bells Heard Through the Leaves"), is another astonishing essay in perception by this master musical psychologist, as well as a grand study in sonority. The entire keyboard is mined for all its possibilities as melodic strands soar above, burrow within, and rumble below the elaborate, rippling figuration that holds sway as the animating force of the music. The big chords that set forth the hazy harmony are heard in every conceivable form, in massive block form high and low on the keyboard, but chiefly broken into arpeggios of extraordinary richness. The overall effect is of the gray and lavender light of an autumn afternoon, through which the melodic phrases lazily drift. Again, Debussy combines sound and sight with rare accuracy and power.

Yet more recondite is the second in the set, *Et la lune descend sur le temple qui fût* (And the Moon Falls over the Temple That Was). In this piece, the orientalism of *Pagodes* has taken on a note of decadence. Built chiefly of massive, dissonant chords, with one melancholy and graceful melodic strand intervening, *Et la lune . . .* is an Asian-flavored nocturne of desperate beauty. It anticipates in its rich fantasy the *Préludes,* notably *"Les sons et les parfums tournent dans l'air du soir,"* from Book I, and the mighty *La terrasse des audiences du clair de lune,* from the second series. When listening to this work it seems best to try to discard conventional ideas of how music is supposed to function: it floats into, then gently out of, hearing, insisting on nothing other than its own moody richness and exoticism.

Debussy recognized that the opulent density of the first two pieces called for a change of pace with the third, which, with *Poissons d'or* (Goldfish), is exactly what he delivers. This tour de force of tone painting captures the movement of goldfish in water with nearly alarming accuracy. Buzzing fast figures, passionate trills, and glittering melodies make their freedom of movement and delicate excitements palpable. Toward the middle section of this fast-moving, acrobatic work is a sequence of chords decorated with grace notes, followed by a more rhythmically rigid phrase in which some kind of primal piscine agitation (mating or feeding) is evident. Yet it is not just the fish one perceives in *Poissons d'or,* but the element in which they move, stirred and disturbed continually by their movements.

The six works that constitute the *Children's Corner* of 1906–8 represent a particularly happy synthesis of means and message. In keeping with his subject, Debussy pares the thick pianistic textures and clotted harmonies of the *Estampes* and both sets of *Images* to a clean, spare simplicity, while in no way stinting on the allusive richness of his music. Inspired by and dedicated to his beloved daughter Chouchou ("with her father's tender excuses for what follows"), these brilliant little sound pictures, despite their economy of means, are far from mere sketches. The composer transfers his psycho-pictorial method to a child's vision of the world, which he re-inhabits with the greatest ease and acuity.

Many streams of inspiration flow into the *Children's Corner.* Schumann's brilliant and well-known *Kinderszenen,* thirteen brief works with which that master captures a child's views, joys, fears, and anxieties, is the most obvious model, but there are forty-three additional pieces for children in the *Album for the Young,* op. 68, with many fine studies, ranging from simple to moderately difficult, among them. Debussy also knew and admired the song cycle *The Nursery* by another great musical psychologist, Modest Mussorgsky. This suite of seven short songs captures the excitements and terrors of a brother and sister talking to their nanny; Mussorgsky assumes the children's identities with a trenchant clarity that is nearly disturbing. Debussy wrote of his deep admiration for this music:

> [Mussorgsky] is quite unique, and will be renowned for an art that suffers from no stultifying rules or artificialities. Never before has such a refined sensibility expressed itself with such simple means. . . . He composes in a series of bold strokes, but his incredible gift of foresight means that each stroke is bound to the next by a mysterious thread. (Lesure 20–21)

Bach may have provided a more abstract example with the works he composed for his children and pupils. These works, notably the *Little Clavier Book of Anna Magdalena Bach* and the two- and three-part Inventions, were designed as technical studies, though they show little in the way of concessions to immature or inexperienced players and there is no assumption on Bach's part of a child's point of view, as with Schumann and Mussorgsky.

Finally, there is Muzio Clementi (1752–1832), the Roman-born piano virtuoso and composer once mentioned in the same breath as Mozart and Beethoven, and currently rehabilitated as a solid third-stringer. Clementi's collection of one hundred technical studies, *Gradus ad Parnassum* (The Steps to Mount Parnassus, home of the muses), remains an important teaching tool for piano students and instructors. This set is the takeoff point for the opening work of the *Children's Corner, Doctor Gradus ad Parnassum*. Written in plain C major, erroneously considered the easiest key in which to play because it lacks sharps or flats—the "black" notes—this wonderful piece opens the set with bustling cheer, directly expressed in a way that is rare in the mature Debussy. The same pure, visceral joy and excitement are also evident in Debussy's other affectionate send-up of piano study, the far more difficult first etude, also in C major and marked *"d'après Monsieur Czerny,"* the composer in that case being the Viennese pedagogue Karl Czerny. The harmony shifts in the middle section, and in its dreamy billowing one can almost feel Debussy stepping away from his idea and looking at it. But the opening soon returns, ending this touching piece on a bright and energetic note.

Jimbo's Lullaby is apparently a tribute to a stuffed elephant that was a favorite of Chouchou's. It opens with a comically awkward passage, for the left hand alone, that delineates Jimbo's clumsy gait or perhaps Chouchou's gestures as she makes him walk. The keyboard texture may be thin, but every note is there, as a delicate and pretty melody enters. The walking bass of the middle section suggests some kind of nursery adventure for Jimbo and his mistress, and the lovely melody plays itself out once more to a charming, spare conclusion low on the keyboard. *Serenade for the Doll* opens with a strumming figure, over and through which a delicate melody winds. The middle section, in which the rhythmic accompaniment is strummed insistently, suggests that Chouchou has perhaps begun to scold her doll, but the composer summons the affectionate tone of the opening to end the work.

As fine as the first three pieces have been, *The Snow Is Dancing* seems a masterpiece of understated wonder, capturing a child's love of snow and fascination with its visual patterns. Debussy achieves these effects with texture, which is of exquisite delicacy throughout, and rhythm, by shifting accents and mixing patterns in a way that evokes the experience of watching snow fall. While keeping the textures simple, Debussy indulges in some striking dissonances that add color to this brilliant tone poem, in which one seems to hear infinite shadings of white and gray.

Harmonic uncertainty is the key to the opening of *The Little Shepherd,* which begins with a sad melody in the right hand that only gradually finds it way home. This is the sound of the shepherd's pipe, much like the one at the beginning of act 3 of Puccini's *Tosca.* This simple piece, free in melody and rhythm, looks ahead to the preludes *La fille aux cheveux de lin* and *Bruyères.*

Last in this wonderful series, and surely the most famous, is *Golliwogg's Cake-walk,* a tribute to a little black doll popular at the time. This energetic little dance is Debussy's first venture into the jazzy rhythms of ragtime; it would be followed in that path by the prelude *Minstrels.* Sharp rhythms, long pauses, and explosive accents set a brisk comic tone. Debussy has fun in the middle section by quoting the languishing opening notes of Wagner's *Tristan und Isolde.* Nothing could be more incongruous than the insertion of that that grave, agonized, rhythmless sequence in the middle of this French takeoff on a black American dance step. The brisk cakewalk returns to bring the wonderful *Children's Corner,* a work that speaks to the heart with rare directness, to its end.

The sweet and languorous *La plus que lente* (The Even Slower Waltz) is a charming work of 1910 with a nearly decadent atmosphere. In it, Debussy mimics and mocks the slow waltzes played by string ensembles at teatime in the cafes and hotel lobbies of fashionable Paris. Yet, for all its parody, *La plus que lente* is beautifully put together; there is real sweep and an emotional center to this fine short work. It has always been popular, if more on the radio or as an encore than as an element of a serious recital program.

The Music for Orchestra After 1900

Two excellent works of smaller dimension stand amid the towering peaks of Debussy's post-1900 works for orchestra. He wrote the *Danses sacrée et profane* for harp and string orchestra in 1904 on a commission from a harp manufacturer. This fine pair, forming a unified whole, elicits from Debussy the solemnity and nostalgia typical of his backward glances into time or musical history; thus they resemble in tone and posture the Sarabande of *Pour le piano* and *Hommage à Rameau*. The *Danse sacrée* has a gravity that anticipates the glorious *Danseuses de Delphes* that opens the first book of preludes. Its companion, which sways to complex rhythmic patterns, foreshadows the intricacies of the late Sonata for Flute, Viola, and Harp. It is "profane" only in ironic comparison to the noble but still graceful tread of the *Danse sacrée*. The dances are well adapted to performance by smaller chamber orchestras, as in the spectacular 1951 recording by harpist Ann Mason Stockton and the Concert Arts Strings under Felix Slatkin's direction.

Perhaps slightly less substantial but no less beautiful is the *Rapsodie no. 1 pour clarinette* of 1910, composed as a competition piece for the Paris Conservatory. The accompaniment, originally for piano, was orchestrated by the composer in 1911. (There is no second rhapsody.) The music alternates between dreamy lyricism and playful athleticism, a contrast well suited to the split personality of this most flexible of the woodwinds. Debussy was fond of the work, calling it "one of the most pleasing pieces I have written" (Lockspeiser 175).

Debussy began his great symphonic work *La mer*—The Sea—in 1902, after the premiere of *Pelléas et Mélisande,* completing it in 1905. *La mer* was first played in October of that year; its obvious merits—

led by a fearsome, raw power—immediately earned for it a secure place in the repertory of major symphonic works. Throughout his life, Debussy spoke of his love for the sea, reminding one friend that his father had once hoped that he might become a sailor (Lockspeiser 193). Debussy also spent summers in direct contact with the North Atlantic on the coast of Normandy, on the Channel Islands, and in the English coastal town of Eastbourne.

Whatever the stimulus that caused him to write it, *La mer* displays the composer's sensitivity to the natural world, and, as in *Nuages* from the *Nocturnes* for orchestra or *Brouillards* from the second book of *Préludes,* his unparalleled ability to depict it musically. *La mer* also shows the composer at the height of his powers, with all elements, from form to theme to orchestration, coming together with a new vigor and an absolute mastery of compositional craft. There is, moreover, a spiritual component in this music at which the composer only hinted before; in *La mer,* Debussy's ecstasy is immanent and overpowering. *La mer* is also the only one of the master's mature multimovement orchestral works in which the movements form a unified whole that may not be disassembled: the three *Nocturnes* may well be played independently with no loss of integrity. Among the orchestral *Images, Ibéria* has always stood apart as the most played of that set, but the three pieces are separate, not forming a single work.

Like most of Debussy's mature works, all three movements of *La mer* have titles that describe in the poor medium of words what the music so stunningly depicts. The first, *De l'aube à midi sur la mer* (From Dawn to Noon on the Sea), opens in the low strings, with harp and tympani evoking the darkness; strings and winds enter, suggesting the movement of the ocean that one hears and feels but cannot yet see. The orchestral colors brighten and grow louder as the sunrise, depicted by a rising figure in the strings and winds, mounts gloriously, then suddenly breaks off. A new rhythmic figure, played by the violins and violas, soon joined by a harp, emerges, paired with a tune for the flutes, clarinets, and cellos, in which the rocking of the waves seems all but palpable: more real, somehow, than any memory of the sea. Harps play a figure in which the spray off the crests of the waves is unmistakable. Muted horns then enter with a strange, hovering melody, perhaps inspired by the image of a seabird on the wing; another lyrical theme enters, sung by the oboe, followed by one for the flutes over plucked strings. Even early in the movement, Debussy does not hold back; the music displays from first to last a pantheistic intensity.

The music quiets down over a couple of moments in which all the themes are played. A solo violin soars languidly above delicately rocking figures in the winds, led by the oboe. As mysteriously as the movements of the ocean, the music reanimates, the strings swirling furiously, followed by chords for the heavy brass, stunningly clear in their depiction of the crashing of bigger waves. This too dies down to a muttering, after which a new, more genial but still sharply accented theme is sung out by the violas and cellos. Through careful redistribution of the new theme's rhythmic pattern, Debussy builds it to a climax, achieving an astonishing depiction of the syncopated collisions of gigantic masses of water.

The clashing rhythms smooth out, and a lyrical moment, beginning with a slow melody for the English horn over quiet strings, develops before the movement's climax. A majestic theme for the bassoons, horns, and one trombone, accompanied by sparkling figuration (again, clearly the sea's briny spray) for the flute and harps marks the heart-stopping closing section, which builds quickly but majestically to a radiant climax—a glittering noon on the ocean, indeed—then to a swift fade-out for the full orchestra. The movement's tremendous culmination is direct in expression and readily understandable by anyone with ears; it looks ahead to the even grander climax of the third movement.

The power of the first and third movements of *La mer* demands a lightening of texture and mood in the central section. Thus *Jeux de vagues* (The Waves at Play) offers a few minutes of grace and ease, if not exactly relaxation. In his program notes to the devastating 1953 performance of *La mer* by the NBC Symphony Orchestra under Arturo Toscanini, William Youngren perceptively describes it as "an extremely cultivated and elegant waltz." Unusually for Debussy, whose view of musical meter was infinitely flexible, so that he changed time signatures often and with ease in many of his works, this movement stays in triple time for its entire length.

Jeux de vagues begins quietly, with shuddering in the strings, above which the winds slither nimbly. This long introduction fades as the infinitely graceful main theme, marked by trills, appears in the violins. Instrumental color is crucial to this movement, in which the harps swoop and the triangle and glockenspiel make crucial contributions. Horns and trumpets chatter, as well, sometimes brightly, often muted, to a more subtle effect. Debussy builds it to a fluent climax as the strings, backed strongly by the trumpet and harps, alternate their statements of the main theme. But, as in the first movement, Debussy imagines a diminution of the sea's endless motion, and he concludes the "game" with a metallic wash of sound, led by the harp, assisted by trumpets, cymbal, and glockenspiel.

The last movement, *Dialogue du vent et de la mer* (Dialogue of the Wind and Sea), begins, like its companions, in darkness, deep in the orchestra on the drums and with the growling of low strings. Debussy makes clear from the outset that godlike forces are here at work. Moaning winds present one of the movement's main themes in a tortured form; muted trumpets cry out in the blackness. The musical gestures are abrupt, with the brass snarling and the percussion and strings playing sharply snapped-off phrases. The tempo slackens a bit to make room for a broad theme in the woodwinds over a surging accompaniment in the strings. The violins play a sharp figure as the low strings and horns chant the trumpets' wild theme, leading to an unimaginably huge climax, with the brass roaring out downward scales that totter, then topple like waves, the very image of a wild gray ocean driven before an irresistible wind.

But there is more to come. With a sense of pacing known only to the greatest masters, Debussy relaxes the tension just a bit to let his listeners breathe and to build the greater moments that are to follow. The horns mutter a variant of the solemn chordal theme first heard in the woodwinds as the violins play a more relaxed accompaniment, suggesting a slight momentary calming of the waves. An abrupt pizzicato for the strings leads to a lightening of the thick orchestral texture as an eerie, almost rhythmless new theme appears in the flutes and oboes, accompanied by the harps and violins producing special hollow tones known as *harmonics,* which the players create by touching the strings very lightly. The woodwind theme moves into a more lyrical, rocking conclusion, which the English horn, accompanied by the glockenspiel, takes up in a final moment of near tranquility in this stunning music, so filled with the restless movement of the sea.

The music hurtles forward as chattering trumpets enter with a sharp, dancelike figure, to which the brassy sound of muted cornets adds a new, metallic color as the strings and winds contest for primacy. The woodwinds pick up the trumpets' rhythmic figure as the flutes and oboes chant the first trumpet tune, then, frantically, the weird theme first played by the high winds. The music pushes toward the end with unbearable urgency as the massive array of brass and winds takes up the strange, floating theme over wild figuration in the strings. In a mystical surrender to the divine elements invoked in the title of the movement, the heavy brass chant the muttered horn theme from earlier in the movement in an incarnation of shattering grandeur, a visionary moment that ranks with those in symphonic works by Mozart, Beethoven, Schubert, or Bruckner. The winds and strings move into a more dancelike figure—this is, after all, one of the dances of God—as the trombones blast out the tortured first trumpet theme, ending the work in the choreographic thundering of the full orchestra.

Immense in conception and flawless in execution, *La mer* places Debussy among the immortals once and for all; certainly none dared call his music feminine or decadent afterward. The potency of Debussy's material is great, but more splendid yet is his deployment of it in a way that perfectly depicts the ocean in its beauty, terrible power, and constant motion.

The three *Images* for orchestra are mature masterpieces that summon inspiration both visual and auditory, with the *Gigues* and *Rondes de printemps* inspired by dance forms, and *Ibéria* an imaginative dramatic scenario of the sights and sounds of an afternoon, night, and morning in Spain. Debussy worked on the three pieces that constitute the series between 1905 and 1912, but *Ibéria* and *Rondes de printemps* received their premiere in 1910; *Gigues* three years later. The title suggests a kinship with the two contemporaneous sets of *Images* for the piano. Indeed, all the music shares a pictorialism that ranges from the abstract patterns of the orchestral *Gigues* and the *Mouvement* that is the third movement of the first series for piano, to the more specific tone-painting of *Reflets dans l'eau* and *Poissons d'or* (for keyboard) and *Ibéria*. In terms of style, *Images* marks a shift from the middle-period fullness of *La mer,* which still echoes clearly in *Ibéria*'s vivid instrumental palette, toward the more delicate style of *Gigues* and *Rondes de printemps,* precursors to the ultimate refinements of instrumental color Debussy was to achieve in the late masterwork *Jeux.*

Debussy apparently composed the three works as musical sketches of three nations. The only one that now seems to have an indisputably national character is *Ibéria,* one of the most convincingly Spanish works in the classical repertoire. It seems wrong to describe *Gigues,* based on the "keel row," a dance from the north of England, as particularly British in character; and although *Rondes de printemps* employs at least two French nursery songs, there is nothing more specifically French about it than anything else Debussy composed.

The *Gigues* of the opening movement are the same lively dance used by Bach as the closing movements of his six suites for solo cello, the E-major Partita for solo violin, and five of the six partitas for keyboard. The easy cognate that is the English translation for *gigue* is "jig," as in the Irish variety, known for characteristic skipping rhythm. There is in Debussy's melancholy, sophisticated dance little of its native North Country roughness; this jig has been re-imagined. The composer begins *Gigues* (as he also would *Jeux*) with a dreamlike introductory passage, from which the primary theme gradually emerges from strange harmonies on the flutes, trumpets, celesta, and strings. The graceful jig theme, sung by the oboe's deeper-toned relative the oboe d'amore, to sound "sweet and melancholy," according to Debussy's direction, telling a great deal about the character of the work. Bassoons enter with a second dance, more vigorous and vulgar. Both are put through various transmutations, building to a big climax followed by a long, slow fadeout to an eerie ending.

Gigues is altogether forward-looking. Among its many anticipations of *Jeux* is its inspired scoring, in which Debussy asks instruments to play unusual sounds—for example the trumpets, which chiefly slither quietly—or in unaccustomed combinations, like those of the harps and light percussion. These instruments Debussy uses in novel and entirely

wonderful fashion as an element of color. Rather than heavily empha-
sizing the beat, he opted for the delicate, often syncopated glitter of
the snare drum, xylophone, cymbals, celesta, and harps; except at the
single big climax, the tympani are silent.

The dances of *Gigues* are a long way from their cheerful roots.
Uneasy and even nightmarish owing to sudden distensions of tempo
and strange, floating harmony that continually threaten the flow of the
dances, *Gigues* is a splendid example of music about music—detached,
ironic, and, in this case, quite disturbing, with the cause of its disturbance a mystery.

The piano preludes *La sérénade interrompue* and *La Puerta del Vino;
Soirée dans Grenade* from *Estampes* (track 5); the two-piano suite
Lindaraja; and the Cello Sonata (tracks 14, 15, and 16) are all so high
in quality that it would be wrong to call *Ibéria* the greatest of Debussy's
Spanish pieces, but it is surely the largest in scale and the most lavish.
The power, brilliance, and beauty of this three-movement work, which
stands as the central triptych within a triptych of the *Images* for orchestra, has found for *Ibéria* a popularity far wider than its companion works
have enjoyed. More frankly pictorial and less emotionally ambiguous
than *Rondes de printemps,* and certainly than *Gigues, Ibéria* is big-boned
and formally satisfying in a way that looks back to *La mer,* with its three
inseparable movements that build toward a cathartic ending.

Debussy gave each movement a descriptive title. The first, *Par les
rues et par les chemins* (In the Streets and Lanes), paints a musical image
of a Spanish town on a bright, hot afternoon. It opens with a magnificent rhythmic gesture, a gigantic snap for the full orchestra, including
castanets, that draws the atmosphere with startling force and clarity.
The clarinets gurgle out a swaying melody that so convincingly mimes
popular Spanish tunes it is hard to believe Debussy did not quote one,
but indeed it is his own invention. Winds and percussion dominate this
opening section, until the violins shriek out the clarinet tune. There is a
change in rhythm as the listener seems to hear, feel—and almost smell—
a variety of comings and goings in this glorious, sun-drenched scene.
But the bits of mystery and intrigue are good-natured and even joyous.

A brilliant fanfare for horns, playfully mimicked by the trumpets,
perhaps depicting the entry of cavalry riders into the scene, open the

second half of the movement. Tension builds as the brass fanfare is submerged under winds and strings, only to reappear cheerfully on the piccolo. The opening returns, now more urgent and dramatic in tone. Harps and strings chase each other playfully, then a discussion between the woodwinds ends this magnificent movement quietly.

Les parfums de la nuit (Scents of the Night) is Debussy's title for the sensuous nocturne that is the center of *Ibéria.* His friend the Spanish composer Manuel de Falla called it an evocation of "the intoxicating spell of Andalusian nights" (Lockspeiser 200)—or perhaps it embodies Cole Porter's "purple light of a summer night in Spain"—and it is indeed a dusky and delicate tone poem that nevertheless carries a hypnotic power. As in *Soirée dans Grenade,* there is a clear sense of several scenes cinematically intercut, with snatches of faraway song floating into hearing, then fading, and an extraordinary evocation, before the midpoint of the movement, of the loud chorus of cicadas, an effect that Bartók later used effectively in several of his most important works, including the second movement of the Piano Concerto no. 3 and the third movement of the *Music for Strings, Percussion, and Celesta.* The final section is an orchestral impression of an impassioned love song, followed by a long, drowsy fade-down.

Debussy connects the second and third movements with a remarkable transitional passage. Following a falling melody in the oboes, the flutes play a phrase in which night can be perceived as fading and the sky lightening; faraway chimes suggest the call of the bells in the church, and there is a distant trumpet call. The last movement, *Le matin d'un jour de fête* (A Festival Morning), breaks in, at first quietly, with the excited march rhythm that will dominate to the end; but first Debussy brilliantly depicts the final moments of the dwindling darkness as the hazy tones of the middle movement come back for just a moment, to be pushed away once and for all by the march theme. Skirling winds, snare drum, and chimes set the stage for the appearance of the main theme of the movement, a startling pizzicato element that is less a traditional melody than a musical picture of guitarists marching in the parade, in which the march rhythm naturally dominates. To achieve this effect, Debussy turns the whole string section into a colossal guitar. While reminiscent of the guitar effects on the piano in *Soirée dans Grenade,* this fierce strumming has a much different effect on the ear—and nervous system—of the listener.

Like one of Mahler's marches, but openhearted and less ironic, the clarinet blares a shrill, vulgar tune, after which rhythmic shifts paint an image of the jostling crowd and of other bands playing in the distance; in a comic moment, a violin solo is pushed rudely aside by winds and percussion. The pace quickens as the big march returns, now played by bowed strings, then plucked by the harps, then plucked by the strings. Debussy raises the excitement to a boil, crushing his themes together and, in a tremendous cinematic moment, having the trombones, whose normal orchestral role tends to be limited to solemn pronunciations, perform wild slides. The music lurches to its massive, powerful end, giving listeners the sense that they are in the very heart of the mob on this hot, bright Spanish morning.

Ibéria's popularity is well deserved. This is a large-scale, tightly crafted masterpiece in which material and means of expression are perfectly aligned. Here, as in all of Debussy's mature works, the ultimate effectiveness of the music depends on rhythm and instrumental color. Themes are repeated by different instruments and in different rhythms, but not developed in the classical sense: at the end of *Le matin d'un jour de fête,* Debussy reiterates his thematic material ever more breathlessly, rather than manipulating it to a triumphant or tragic apotheosis. Debussy basically changed the rules of composition with works like *Ibéria,* constructed differently than the symphonic standards but manifestly great on its own terms. An interesting historical footnote is the composition of the well-known and splendid suite for piano of the same name at the same time by the Spanish composer Isaac Albéniz (1860–1909). Debussy knew the piece but draws on it in his work not at all.

The *Rondes de printemps* (Rounds of Spring) returns to the more abstract musical imagery of *Gigues,* but with an infinitely lighter heart. The "rounds" referred to in the title are old-fashioned round dances. Again, the harmony and orchestration are of high sophistication, but the tonal colors are light, with a kind of pale green feeling appropriate to the subject. The *Rondes* opens with a long introduction in which winds trade phrases over shimmering strings and harp; the dance impulse manifests itself early, although in an unformed way. Once again, Debussy calls on the harps to function as light percussion, working in tandem with the hanging cymbal and triangle. The first main theme is of a rare rhythmic complexity, and melody and accompaniment are here inseparable.

Another tune with a more traditional springlike lilt is first stated gracefully (marked by Debussy to be played "with charm") by the flutes and clarinets. Another series of elegant calls pass from oboe to English horn to the French horn, then restated with sour harmony reminiscent of the harsh voices of nestling birds. The music moves ahead with great fluidity, pausing occasionally to shimmer as though in the uncertain spring sun. As always, Debussy asks orchestral underlings to take center stage, as in the swift but striking passages for the bassoons near the end. The conclusion is an exciting episode in which the full orchestra is heard is briefly in all its glory but, ideally, with absolute clarity, as well. Less a dance piece than a study of spring sounds and feelings, the *Rondes de printemps* is a refined work of the highest quality that deserves frequent performance and careful listening.

Written as a ballet in 1912 on a commission from the choreographer Vaslav Nijinsky, *Jeux* (Games) is one of the great masterpieces of Debussy's late period. *Jeux* has rarely been performed as a ballet, and its subtlety and sophistication make it an unlikely crowd-pleaser, but those qualities have earned for it the deepest admiration of musicians and knowledgeable audiences. Sounding like nothing else, this feat of compositional virtuosity is not easy to grasp for the first several hearings but offers abundant rewards for the patient listener.

Nijinsky's slim scenario opens in a deserted park, into which a tennis ball bounces, followed by the young man to whom it belongs. As he departs, two "timid and curious" girls enter with secrets to share, but the beauty of the night stimulates them to dance. The tennis player returns, frightening the girls at first but quickly calming them as he dances with one girl. The second is jealous, but he soon dances with her, then all three together; at the climax, "the young man, with a passionate gesture, has drawn their heads together . . . and a triple kiss mingles them in one ecstasy." Suddenly, another tennis ball falls at their feet, as all three flee in fright. That the premise of this trite *ménage-à-trois* stimulated Debussy's imagination to the creation of a score so fantastically rich seems incredible; such are the mysteries of genius.

Jeux opens with a long introductory passage that begins slowly and mysteriously, then shudders into life with a very modern-sounding display of glittering thematic fragments scattered with the utmost care across the instrumental groups, including the xylophone, cymbals, and tambourine. A slithering downward run in the violins precedes a bouncing figure for winds and strings in which the sound of the unseen tennis game can be heard. The slow passage is repeated with strange sonorities in the strings as the body of the work proper begins, with a theme, distributed among the woodwinds, that runs throughout the work. The effect is of a vast, breathtaking mosaic of instrumental sounds. The young man's first appearance is to a waltz-like theme. The girls appear to giddy trills in the violins, accented by grace notes in the trumpets. An important theme is heard in the violins as the music moves ahead steadily through both girls' dances.

The young man's dance, a beautiful, slow waltz, is notable for its schmaltzy Viennese lilt and the strange sonority of trumpets that mark its high point. His pairing with the first girl swoons with ironic passion, and the reaction of the second is portrayed in dry, light phrases for violins and flutes, joined eventually by the chortling of two bassoons. The dance with the second girl starts with another fantastically energetic passage in waltz rhythm; their *pas de deux* is marked by a passage in which the woodwinds sweep and swoop, marked by Debussy to be played "with joy." In the dance for all three, a passage that blends passion with musical density, the main theme of the work (first played by the woodwinds) is sung out richly by the cellos, then all the strings. The dance builds to a climax marked "violent"; it is possible to hear in it a sexual rhythm and, in the dying rhythms and thinning sonority of the succeeding passage, a postcoital calm. The lovers scatter to notes for harp, light percussion, and strings that seem barely there; the last two pages bring back the opening passage, with an eerie figure for violins and violas, and the work concludes on a sly three-note hiccup for the whole orchestra.

Making its formidable case on sheer sound, the variety of instrumental combinations in *Jeux* is astonishing. Debussy also employs in it his most advanced harmonic thinking, another obstacle to broader popularity. But what strikes the listener above all about *Jeux* is its lightness and delicacy: for all the orchestra's size, the writing is utterly clear and the climaxes, although thick, are swift. Because of its complexity, *Jeux* is particularly gratifying to follow with the score, where the progress of Debussy's imagination can be followed as with a road map. Fine-boned but intense, *Jeux* casts a long shadow over twentieth-century music, with its influence audible in the work of every subsequent composer worth hearing, including Bartók, Stravinsky, Varèse, Milhaud, Honegger, Maderna, Messiaen, and Boulez.

There are three other late works for large orchestral forces that are rarely or never heard but require mention; curiously, Debussy left the orchestration of all three to others. The most successful of these, *La boîte à joujoux* (The Toybox), a "children's ballet" of 1913, has much to offer but is on the light side and is rarely performed. The main character is a toy soldier of the British Grenadiers, and the sparkling five-movement work contains a battle, a comically elephantine dance, and a cakewalk. Orchestrated by the composer's friend and aide André Caplet, it is in much the same spirit as the *Children's Corner*. With a playing time of over thirty minutes, *La boîte à joujoux* is perhaps just a bit light in substance for a symphonic concert. But the music is fine, and more frequent performances would surely be welcome.

The Canadian dancer Maud Allan commissioned the ballet *Khamma*, an elaborate retelling of an ancient Egyptian myth, in 1912. Needing cash as always, Debussy accepted the project. He wrote most of the score, which was completed and orchestrated by Charles Koechlin, another acolyte. Here is a rare example of subpar effort by the mature composer, who was sick and who must have had other work on his mind. The material lacks the sparkle of its contemporary, *Jeux*, and Koechlin's heavy-handed orchestration does little to remedy that shortcoming.

Finally, there is the strange hybrid that is *Le martyre de St Sébastien*, on which the composer worked briefly but intensely and which is nothing if not problematic. Composed over a couple of months in 1911, *Le martyre* was ambitiously conceived as a "mystery play," modeled on medieval religious drama. Its originator was the dancer Ida Rubinstein, who engaged Debussy, the Italian writer Gabriele d'Annunzio, and the Russian set designer Léon Bakst for the prestigious project. Its purpose was to retell the story of Sebastian, the Roman captain whom the emperor had killed by the arrows of his archers, a Christian retelling of the classical myth of Adonis. Rubinstein herself choreographed and performed the work, which the Archbishop of Paris promptly forbade Catholics to see.

Thus, in its original form, *Le martyre* involved, music, dance, and spoken narration. It is unclear whether the work, which was poorly received, has ever been performed again in that form. This difficulty with form demanded adaptations, from four "symphonic fragments," to an hour-plus version in which it is presented, more or less complete, as an oratorio. The fragment form is rarely heard anymore, which is probably for the best. Like the full oratorio, the four instrumental interludes lack variety in tone and pacing, but more conspicuously without the textural changes bestowed by soloists and chorus. Although the requirements for three solo vocalists, chorus, and a narrator make the oratorio version harder for an orchestra to put together, it is infinitely more satisfying in all ways.

The music for *Le martyre,* which the normally slow and deliberate Debussy assembled in just a few weeks, is uneven. The influence of Wagner's last opera, *Parsifal,* which deals with similar issues of lust, faith, doubt, and redemption, has long been noted as an influence; the slow, stately pacing of *Le martyre* does indeed resemble that of Wagner's final, sublime work. Debussy's reliance on Wagner is uncharacteristically evident in many musical details, as well. Certainly the brassy, thumping prelude to the third part does not show Debussy at his best.

But everything written by this great composer in the flush of his maturity has some merit, and *Le martyre* has its share of wonderful moments. The entire opening part is fine, from the prelude through the sad, solemn duet of the condemned brothers Mark and Marcellian, and Sebastian's strange, ecstatic dance. Debussy's reliance on Wagner is more evident in the second part, the prelude to which clearly draws on that of act 2 of *Parsifal.* But this music speaks in Debussy's own harmonic and instrumental idioms. Other high points include the eerie accompaniment to the words of the narrator and the choruses of the women of Byblos in the third part, and its marvelously strange final chorus (*Il est mort, le bel Adonis*). Even though *Le martyre* is indefensible against charges of unevenness, the piece certainly has its own atmosphere and aesthetic.

The problems with *Le martyre de St Sébastien* can safely be attributed to the pressure under which Debussy wrote the music. Given more time, he surely would have adjusted some tempos for variety and purged the more obvious Wagnerian influences, as he did with *Pelléas*.

Pour le Piano III:
The Preludes

D ebussy's two sets of preludes represent the summit of his achievement as a composer for the piano. Every one of these twenty-four pieces is a masterwork, with some ranking among the composer's most beautiful and revolutionary compositions.

The title "prelude" may suggest incompleteness, with a listener expecting it to prepare the way for something else, such as a fugue, as with Bach and Shostakovich, or miniaturization, as with Chopin, whose works of that title are indeed mostly very short, although extraordinarily dense, as well. But Debussy's adoption of a title used by two of the masters he most revered has other significances.

Following a different path, Debussy conceived his preludes as independent pieces of moderate length, with the shortest typically taking a bit over two minutes to play, and the longest—*La cathédrale engloutie*—somewhere between five and seven. Most of Chopin's preludes vary widely, even wildly, in duration, with several taking no more than half a minute and the longest by far (no. 15 in D-flat major) being about five minutes long. Their short duration permits many of Chopin's preludes to be correctly called miniatures without disparagement of the intensity of their content. But playing time says nothing at all about Debussy's preludes, none of which remotely fit the description of miniatures: whereas some, like *Des pas sur la neige* (Footsteps in the Snow), are quiet and intimate, these works are large in scope and musical character, as wise pianists have long understood. No player in his right mind would treat the massive *La cathédrale engloutie* as a miniature, but even the shortest prelude, the two-minute *Le vent dans la plaine* (The Wind on the Plain), is big-boned and fierce.

In Debussyan terms, the title "prelude" is neutral, exerting less pull on the listener than obviously visual titles like *Images* or *Estampes*. But, as with the nine individual works of which the *Estampes* and the two mature sets of the *Images* for piano are constituted, each prelude was granted by the composer a title that is suggestive, if not strictly descriptive. Most of the works depict the aural images suggested by the titles, and a few are studies of characters from literature or, in one case, a sketch of a performer Debussy knew. *La cathédrale engloutie* recounts a legend; only *Les tierces alternées* from Book II is based on a purely technical idea, that of alternating thirds, which actually make for interesting aural patterns as well as patterns on the printed page. Most baffling of all the titles is *"Les sons et les parfums tournent dans l'air du soir"* ("Sounds and Scents Turn on the Evening Air"), a line from a Baudelaire poem Debussy admired. The mysteriously named prelude is neither musical picture nor portrait, nor legend, but another attempt by the composer to capture the vague, indirect, darting effects in the memory of sounds, sights, and feeling.

The visual aptness of the preludes is obvious when listening to them, but it is also important for the interested listener to understand that Debussy seems to have developed his musical ideas before titling the pieces. The titles are, significantly, given at the end of each work, rather that at the head, in the beautifully printed editions of the preludes by Debussy's original publisher, Durand. This placing of the titles is important because it is Debussy's way of telling the player that the pieces are music, first and foremost.

Debussy composed the first set of preludes in late 1909 and early 1910; they were published in the latter year. Given the length and complexity of some, the dates sometimes indicated as those on which he composed each work are likelier their dates of completion. In any case, Debussy, at the height of his powers, worked on them with speed and assurance. He also took pains in placing them in the best sequence for aesthetic, cathartic release and effectiveness in performance. Unlike Chopin's preludes, which follow the unalterable path of the twenty-four keys in the harmonic structure known as the circle of fifths, Debussy composed each prelude in the key in which he imagined it. His two sets are carefully and effectively structured, with clear senses of opening, rise, fall, and closing. Performances of the complete sets therefore make artistic sense and have been the general, though not the absolute, rule, almost from the beginning.

The first volume opens with *Danseuses de Delphes* (Delphic Dancers), one of the grandest and most impressive of all the preludes. Debussy's inspiration for the piece was a sculpted column in the Louvre in the form of a female image that reminded him of dancers moving in grave worship of the god Apollo (Roberts 243). Although only thirty-one measures long, the slow tempo pushes the playing time of the piece to about three minutes; yet it is so spacious and magnificent that it cannot sensibly be regarded as a miniature. *Danseuses de Delphes* opens with a majestic phrase that rises in the right hand over one that gently descends in the left, immediately presenting the delicate dissonance (a major second) that pervades the piece and on which its peculiar rich, dusty sound is based. A second phrase, in a different, billowing rhythm and with repeated chords and solemn harmony, seems to frame the opening and comment on it. The opening themes are repeated in varied forms, after the rising theme is reinterpreted higher on the keyboard, and this time in falling form. Massive chords, far apart on the keyboard, sound majestically in strange, remote harmonies, imparting a sense of gravity and distance—perhaps distance in time—yet for all its stateliness, the music seems to float. There is another series of thoughtful chords, again in faraway harmonies offering the sort of quiet commentary from outside so typical of Debussy, and this great work seems about to fade away on broken phrases drawn from throughout the work when a rich chord is sounded loudly, then repeated quietly in a striking conclusion. The many points of view from which Debussy examines his material are but one of the many complexities of this majestic and beautiful work.

The ambiguities of *Voiles,* the second prelude, begin before a note is sounded. The French word means both "sails" and "veils." Early interpreters felt strongly that the work clearly suggested a view of ships sailing on a blue ocean on a sunny day; later critics claim that Debussy was inspired by the artistry of Loïe Fuller, a dancer famous for using large veils in her work. It does seems easier to picture the gentle floating of veils than a day at the shore in the harmonic daring of this very modern music, but both interpretations may be wrong, or simply too specific.

Whether it's about a boat or a veil, this music floats. Using what is known as a whole-tone scale—which consists of only six notes instead of the usual twelve—then later a pentatonic scale, which has only five, Debussy steers *Voiles* away from any sense of a home key. This unusual harmonic scheme, as well as the fluid rhythm and gentle dynamics, with only one passage rising above a murmur, are what give the piece its floating quality. Debussy's indications to the performer are highly unusual but instructive about the hazy, gauzy sound he was after: the tempo indication is *modéré*—moderate, with the further comment "in a rhythm that is caressing and without rigor." Over the last two lines are written "very calm and attenuated to the end." Since understanding of this strange, extraordinarily beautiful music cannot be forced, it seems wisest to let it drift over one until it begins to make sense, which it eventually does, though entirely on its own extralogical terms.

The third prelude, *Le vent dans la plaine* (The Wind on the Plain), creates the strongest contrast imaginable with *Voiles*. Here, sharply accented notes combine with a figure in a musical impression of the howling and snarling of the wind. Little chords shudder delicately down the keyboard, suggesting leaves scurrying over the ground, or perhaps across the surface of a pond. A splendid but brief chordal outburst in the middle has overwhelming power and drama in the midst of all the soft, fast-moving passagework. The piece dies away as though the wind has abruptly moved on. This swift, spooky prelude is the little brother of the even more terrifying *Ce qu'a vu le vent d'ouest* (What the West Wind Saw), which comes seventh in this first set.

The title of the fourth prelude, "*Les sons et les parfums tournent dans l'air du soir*," appears in quotation marks because it is quoted from the poem *Harmonie du soir* (Evening Harmony) of Charles Baudelaire; it is the only literary work among the preludes, and one of the few in Debussy's output, to receive this honor. The line describes a fusion of the senses called *synesthesia*, much beloved of both poet and composer. This decadent and gorgeous work represents one of Debussy's attempts to capture the drift of sense and feeling through the memory, a depiction in tone of how the mind reviews recent experience. As such, "*Les sons . . .*" is considered one of the most important of all twenty-four preludes and perhaps one of the composer's pivotal works. As the pianist and writer Paul Roberts puts it in *Images,* his study of the visual inspiration in Debussy's piano music, "To appreciate '*Les sons et les parfums tournent dans l'air du soir*' is to hold the key to a central aspect of Debussy's genius" (71).

Debussy puts everyone off base at the start of "*Les sons . . .*" by employing, then immediately dropping, an unusual rhythm that is difficult for the pianist to play and almost impossible for listeners to grasp. It does, however, contain the seed of a waltz-like theme that appears a bit later. Booming notes in the bass and an ascending figure create a rich haze through which the melodic fragments rise and fall. The waltz appears, but not clearly, as though recalled rather than actually heard. This idea is pursued, slowly but at some length, before the strange opening returns. Some new material, notably a forceful downward arpeggio, then a beautiful passage in a steady rhythm marked to be played in a "tranquil and floating" manner, pulls the work toward its ending. This astonishing phrase is marked by a return of the booming bass notes that opened the work and a faraway motto marked "like a distant horn call." The mock horn call is then repeated with Debussy's injunction to make it sound "yet more distant and held back."

Debussy's expressive markings in "*Les sons . . .*" are uncommonly specific. But despite the clarity of his instructions, and the hints one may want to take from these, and the "horn calls" and booming notes deep on the keyboard, it is unwise to apply a story to this music. It is one of the most accurate depictions of the darting and spiraling of the human mind, but not a picture of a day at the fair, or some such. As in *Voiles,* Debussy has imbued "*Les sons . . .*" with a floating feeling, which in the former work is light, as though stirred by delicate movements of the air, but here is deeply sensuous, and perhaps erotic. Without question, "*Les sons et les parfums tournent dans l'air du soir*" is music of the flesh.

So, in its very different fashion, is the fifth prelude, *Les collines d'Anacapri* (The Hills of Anacapri), the eighth track on the compact disc that accompanies the book. Anacapri is the name of one of the two little towns on Capri, the exquisite island in the Bay of Naples that has since antiquity been a favorite resort of all with the good sense and means to get there. This brightest of the preludes of Book I is a fantastic example of Debussy's skill at creating a musical image that captures the feel of a place with great precision and brilliance. Although his Spanish pieces, particularly *Soireé dans Grenade* (track 5) are well known and popular, the musical profile of *Les collines d'Anacapri* is just as strong, even if the local details differ.

Two of the four ideas that form the prelude are set forth at the beginning: the bell-like chiming sequence that opens the work, followed at 0:08 by the little snatch in the rhythm of the tarantella, marked by Debussy to be "lively, light, and distant." As in *Soirée dans Grenade*, the listener seems to hear bits of sound wafted on the air. The chiming is repeated at 0:14, with the tones left ringing atmospherically. Sharply accented arpeggiated chords (0:25) speed up the pace as the tarantella begins in earnest over a burbling accompaniment at 0:36. As with the habanera of *Soireé dans Grenade*, Debussy has not composed a real tarantella, but rather an image, a memory, or an impression of one. A second dance theme appears in a deeper register at 0:49, before breaking upward into brighter sounds. This idea gives way at 0:59 to a long-spun tune in the left hand, which Debussy asks to be played "with the freedom of a popular song," a hint as to its character if one were needed. The tune bursts out in full, sunlit glory at 1:12, ending in another one of the sharply snapped chords that form a key part of the prelude's musical texture (1:17).

A transitional passage with tremendous gravitational pull (1:22) leads to the fourth and last theme, another popular tune (1:28), this one more earthy and vulgar than the one that came before. Thick with emotion, this mock-Neapolitan street tune can be heard sandwiched within, and sometimes nearly smothered beneath its accompaniment. Here, as before, the listener seems to hear it from a distance, mingled with other noises. It slows, then fragments, as the tarantella brightly returns at 2:18. The first popular song returns in a blaze of glory at 2:39, ending in one last sharply bitten-off chord (2:44) as the music breaks into dissonant fragments that sparkle as though sun-drenched, and the music leaps toward the end in two different rhythms (2:55) that give off sparks as they clash. The last line, marked "luminous," ends the work in one of the most dazzling blazes of light in the musical universe. Debussy developed this magnificent peacock's tail of piano sound—which he also used at the end of *Jardins sous la pluie*, seven years earlier—from Chopin, whose Mazurka in D Major, op. 33, no. 3, is the likely model for both.

There is no more stark expression of loneliness and desolation than *Des pas sur la neige* (Footsteps in the Snow), the hushed, nearly motionless sixth prelude, which represents the center of gravity of the first book. As with *Voiles* and several other preludes, its title contains ambiguities: are the steps heard or, even more bleakly, seen, as tracks of people who have passed from the scene? Debussy does not tell us. Instead listeners must follow him through two pages of agonized slow music that can easily be stretched in performance to nearly five minutes' duration. One of the composer's most stark conceptions for the keyboard, *Des pas sur la neige* is simple to play, but its painful emotional content makes heavy demands on the concentration of player and audience alike.

The prelude opens with a softly muttered phrase, endlessly repeated, over which sighing melodic phrases rise and fall. As usual, Debussy's guides to speed and expression are remarkably clear: he gives the tempo as "slow and sad," with the added injunction that the opening rhythmic figure "should have the aural value of a sad, frozen landscape." A sequence of hollow, falling chords drags the melody downward, but it struggles back to life, albeit at the same crawling pace. Another point of rest is reached on a block-like dissonant chord that shows how much Debussy learned from the Russian master Mussorgsky, as the melody limps into motion once again. This middle section features more big, very dissonant chords, over which the melody pulls to a short-breathed climax, filled with sorrow. The drooping tune starts up yet again, this time over sour dissonances, leading into a new passage, marked "like a tender and sad regret," in which a rising melodic line set over sighing chords pulls away, almost as from a separate consciousness, to comment on what went before. Another few measures of near motionlessness end this extraordinary work in icy, cosmic despair.

The contrast between the stillness of *Des pas sur la neige* and the mad turbulence of *Ce qu'a vu le vent d'ouest* (What the West Wind Saw) that follows could not be greater. It is, of course, calculated: Debussy put considerable care into the ordering of these pieces, with the sixth, seventh, and eighth—the famous "Girl with the Flaxen Hair"—forming what the pianist and writer Paul Roberts has correctly perceived as the central arch of the whole structure of Book I:

> The power of the group comes from the diversity within it: no other preludes of the first book are more dramatically contrasted than these three. Here we have a triptych representing what we might see as crisis, catharsis, and redemption—or in terms of the sensibility of the music, desolation, violence, and tenderness. (252)

Further heightening the contrast of the virtuosic *Ce qu'a vu le vent d'ouest* with its neighbors, the preludes that flank it are also the easiest to play of all twenty-four.

There is no mistaking the cathartic violence of *Ce qu'a vu le vent d'ouest* or its technical inspiration in the music of Franz Liszt, the German composer of Hungarian parentage. Like many composer-pianists of the nineteenth century, Liszt conceived many (though far from all) of his own keyboard works as showpieces to highlight his heroic skills as a player. And only a player of heroic ability dare tackle the enormous difficulties of *Ce qu'a vu le vent d'ouest,* from the sweeping arpeggios that open the work to the thunderous chords and rapid, difficult passagework that carry it through to its shuddering final dissonance. Nor is it possible to confuse this terrifying, godlike wind of myth and legend with the gusts that blow the leaves and rattle the doors—alarming though they may be—of *Le vent dans la plaine.*

With the eighth prelude, *La fille aux cheveux de lin* (The Girl with the Flaxen Hair), Debussy finally gives his listeners some much-needed relief between the static bleakness of *Des pas sur la neige* and the terrors of *Ce qu'a vu le vent d'ouest.* In their place, he offers calm lyricism and genuine warmth that is rare in music of this quality. Nor is detailed musical analysis called for. The famous opening melody, decidedly tonal in is three-note phrases, falls and rises gently, with Debussy stroking the same notes tenderly. It comes firmly to rest at 0:10 on a solid, basic chord, the like of which was not heard in any of the preceding preludes, followed by a falling melodic tail in the same rhythm. At 0:16 the second half of the melody appears, much in the character of a Scottish ballad or a melody by the Norwegian composer Edvard Grieg.

The opening tune returns at 0:31, clothed in a new harmony, then runs itself out at 0:42. A new melodic expansion comes at 0:48, ending in a droning phrase with more strong Scottish flavor at 0:57. The melody soars upward again, reaching a high note at 1:06, then falls gracefully; it mounts steadily to its biggest climax on a turn at 1:28 before falling yet again. There is another calmly droning passage at 1:38, after which the slowly flowing coda begins at 1:54. The opening tune floats in a higher register, the droning passage returns one last time (2:12), and a gently rising passage in the right hand (2:20) brings *La fille aux cheveux de lin* to its end, high on the keyboard.

This wonderful music is understandably popular, consisting of a great and memorable tune over the mellowest accompaniment imaginable. But it is precisely because what has gone before is so challenging that *La fille aux cheveux de lin* is exactly the right piece for its place in Book I of the *Préludes*. Debussy wrote a technically easy, sweetly melodious piece for this spot because he understood the difficulty, pianistically and emotionally, of what came before.

The inspiration of *La sérénade interrompue* (The Interrupted Serenade) is another of Debussy's imaginative Spanish scenarios. In the opening bars, the pianist performs a witty imitation of a guitarist strumming his instrument and tuning up: the score is marked "quasi guitarra" and "like a prelude." The strumming continues at some length, then a parodied voice enters with a wailing, monotonous, but passionate melody that later breaks out into more elaborate descant. Then the first interruption, in the form of another tune of completely different character, elicits a furious response marked *rageur*—angrily—from the serenader, who picks up his strumming and singing once more as the prelude shudders down to a crisp but quiet conclusion. What is remarkable about *La sérénade interrompue* is the elegance and sharpness of Debussy's observation of Spanish popular music and his uncanny ability to create its aural image. Yet, as with all Debussy's renderings of music at a distance—whether Spanish, Italian, Oriental, or folk—he is not trying to re-create or even copy his model, but rather to rehear it. The little comic scene created in this prelude is a brilliant stroke of musical illusion—there is neither guitar nor singer, but magically, the listener perceives both.

The last word in the title of the tenth prelude, *La cathédrale engloutie,* is translated both as "submerged" and "engulfed." Debussy's inspiration in composing this well-known piece is a Breton myth about an ancient cathedral of Ys, drowned, as in the biblical story of Noah's flood, because of the impiety of the town's inhabitants, but allowed to rise from the sea at dawn, as an example to others (Schmitz 155). In this colossal work there is only pure power, with no hint of the "fairy-dust" Debussy. Its characteristic hollow sound and spooky medieval atmosphere are founded on Debussy's persistent use of fourths and fifths, harmonic intervals out of common use since the eleventh century and forbidden by textbooks on composition since the eighteenth. *La cathédrale engloutie* is often described as a musical equivalent to Monet's paintings of the exterior of Rouen Cathedral. The comparison is valid, with Debussy's sound seeming to shimmer off the hard surfaces of the keys and strings, much as Monet's images capture the refraction of light off the cathedral stone.

No other music sounds like *La cathédrale engloutie.* It moves from a quiet opening in strange chords, which range regally over the keyboard, to an even weirder bell-like passage. Once again, Debussy's expressive markings are extraordinary and worth noting: "profoundly calm, in a sweetly sonorous haze." The opening returns, followed by grand chords building over powerful octaves in the left hand. The awe-inspiring main theme, built of massive chords over booming notes in the bass, thunders out with the utmost grandeur; Debussy instructs that it be played "sonorously without hardness." This theme plays itself out in glinting, far-flung notes as a second theme appears deep in the keyboard. This theme reaches its own climax, darker-hued and less titanic than the first, the return of which is presaged by rumblings in the bass. The first theme's recurrence is stately, but the work ends on massive, gently stroked chords.

Recordings of *La cathédrale engloutie* vary significantly in duration, with Alfred Cortot's 1949 performance running a brisk 4:30 and Polish pianist Krystian Zimerman's version coming in at a very broad 7:27. The reason for this wide range of playing times is that the printed music does not show two doublings of tempo—speedings up—that Debussy himself employed when performing the work. These quicker rates can be readily perceived in his own rendition (which runs for 5:01), made in 1913 on a piano roll. This turn-of-the-twentieth-century mechanical device gives almost no feel for nuance but appears to be accurate in performance tempo. Cortot speeds up where the composer does, but few others do, including greats like Michelangeli and Claudio Arrau. Debussy and Cortot's way, unsurprisingly, works better, providing far clearer proportions for the piece and keeping it from dragging, which it tends to do when played entirely at the slow tempo.

Debussy's shrewd sense of drama and pacing served him well when ordering the preludes of Book I. The lighthearted choreographic pair that ends the set contrasts utterly in tone and style with the massive *La cathédrale engloutie.* Both are wonderful pieces. The fantastical *La danse de Puck* (Puck's Dance), a study based on the elf of *A Midsummer Night's Dream,* sashays along in a charmingly unpredictable skipping rhythm; in a marvelous passage marked "airily," Puck seems to hover visibly before the listener. At the end he buzzes away on a long, delicate scale. Debussy's reputation as a great writer of fairy music is founded on *La danse de Puck,* among other works. *Minstrels,* along with *Golliwogg's Cake-walk,* is one of Debussy's marvelous tributes to the jerky rhythms of ragtime and early jazz, and the black American minstrel shows that were immensely popular in Paris around 1900. Witty caricatures of the banjo and cornet open the work, and of the drum (marked "Quasi Tambouro") about three quarters of the way through, then right before the end. Another passage, marked to be played "mockingly," suggests a sentimental song or, in the opinion of one critic, a corny joke (Schmitz 161). One phrase that strongly suggests a shuffling dance appears, then returns clothed in strange harmony. Throughout, the rhythm moves with almost feline tension; some passages are smooth, while others accurately capture the rawness of these entertainments. The work hurries to an almost fierce ending on two jazzy chords.

From ancient Greece to Capri to Spain, to medieval Brittany; across landscapes that are spiritual, hazy, frozen, and windy, the Book I preludes constitute one of the great cyclical works in Western music. The range of Debussy's inspiration and refinement of his technique are stunning, but even more remarkable are his metabolic conversion of far-flung sources through a prismatic imagination. *Minstrels* brings the set to an American-flavored conclusion that is comical, thrilling, perfect. The range, depth, and power of the dozen pieces seem epic, and their forty minutes' playing time seems impossibly brief, given the musical, intellectual, and emotional richness of the music.

Book II, composed three years later, stands at nearly the same exalted level. The parallels between the two sets are many and obvious: there are pieces based on Spanish musical scenes and characters from English literature; ancient artifacts and popular theatrical revues. Fog replaces the winds of Book I, and *Bruyères* (Heather) has the Scottish tang that characterizes *La fille aux cheveux de lin*. There is fairy music in both, and in place of the strange majesty of *La cathédrale engloutie* there is the even weirder and grander *La terrasse des audiences du clair de lune* (The Terrace for Moonlight Audiences; track 11 on the compact disc), one of Debussy's supreme conceptions. Debussy's reliance in Book II on models he had created in Book I makes the later group less original as a set, but the quality of the music is just as high.

Brouillards (Fog; track 10 on the CD), which opens the set, is one of the greatest of all the preludes and another of Debussy's utterly aston-ishing works. It opens with spooky figuration in the right hand over very plain chords in the left. Each hand plays in a different key, creating a profound musical disorientation. There is, moreover, no melody here in the conventional sense, although a rising chord sequence first heard at 0:05 serves as a kind of aural landmark. The music moves steadily until 0:27, when a series of notes emerges above, then below the chords and figuration. As before, this is in no sense a conventional melody, but rather a thematic landmark. The notes, chords, and figuration pulse toward a resting point at 0:43, after which a new theme appears at 0:50 in unison octaves, far apart on the keyboard. Although the most memo-rable idea (from a conventional standpoint) that Debussy has offered yet, this eerie theme presents listeners' puzzled ears with a welcome change in texture and rhythm. One might hear in this taut theme the primal terror that prickles at the back of one's neck when peering blindly into the billowing indeterminateness of the fog. The foggy figuration and plain chords return (1:00), with the eerie theme following; at 1:10 an altered version of the opening returns, sounding as though a breeze is causing the curtain of fog to shift. A more grandly sweeping change in the texture of the swiftly moving arpeggios suggests once more that the fog is moving before a stronger wind, which stops at 1:25 and 1:29, then picks up once more. The opening figuration, now broken into wider arpeggios, moves steadily over broken chords below, suggesting the streaming of the fog (1:34 through 1:55). The eerie theme is heard once more in the left hand, after which another big arpeggio propels the musical fog into a new configuration. The wailing theme comes back (2:04) in the left hand in an abbreviated and condensed version as the music begins to break gently apart. The opening figure and chords come back in fragments (2:14 and on); the rising chords that were the first landmark come back one last time at 2:32, and the piece vanishes, to Debussy's marking "almost inaudibly," on an arpeggio and two little chords (2:36 to the end).

It took great precision on Debussy's part to create the sense of mystery and disorientation one experiences when listening to *Brouillards*: every note adds to its uncanny atmosphere, and in its tightly woven fabric are no extra notes, either. Puzzling as the music may be at first, its sovereign, shimmering beauty, as of light and motion refracted through the mist, is readily apparent after only a few hearings. A feline suppleness of rhythm, a stern rejection of conventional melodic ideas, and a matchless boldness in harmony expressed in dissonances of fearful intensity are the keys to the greatness of this majestic evocation of fog and mist.

As attentive listeners to the preludes will have come to expect, *Feuilles mortes* (Dead Leaves) presents a marked contrast, as well as a logical dramatic and philosophical continuation. This autumnal tone poem lacks the descriptive clarity of *Brouillards*. It is not a musical picture of rustling dead leaves, but an emotional document filled with pain and regret. It consists of three sections: a rich and dark opening, marked by hand crossings and frequent changes of meter; a more mobile, rhythmically alert middle portion; and a return to the grave beginning. Like so many of these pieces, *Feuilles mortes* seems to fade out rather than end conclusively.

The essential Spanish element provided in Book I by *La sérénade interrompue* is supplied here by *La Puerta del Vino* (The Gate of Wine). The work was supposedly inspired by a postcard sent to Debussy by the Spanish composer Manuel de Falla showing one of the gates to the Alhambra palace in Granada, where gypsies assemble. This smoldering portrait of southern Spanish song, dance, and atmosphere shares more with *Soirée dans Grenade* than with its companion prelude, although both contain brilliant imitations of the sinuous Moorish melodic line of the gypsy *cante jondo* and flamenco.

Dance and song are powerfully expressed in *La Puerta del Vino*. Debussy's direction to the performer at the head of the work—one of the most splendid in any musical composition—reads, "with sudden oppositions of extreme violence and passionate tenderness." The work opens with a forceful statement of the same habanera rhythm, tense but infinitely flexible, already familiar from *Soirée dans Grenade,* which continues obsessively through the entire prelude. A moaning melodic line, like that of a flamenco singer, enters above, soon embellished with long, impassioned runs. A second theme, first in narrow melodic phrases, trailed by big, smoky chords, comes next; then the opening figure with a new melodic phrase, ecstatic and filled with pain, is played four times with a different feeling in each iteration. Arpeggios in another one of Debussy's great guitar imitations are marked to be played "ironically," then "graciously," further indications of the expressive intensity of *La Puerta del Vino*. The closing section, not unlike those of *Brouillards* and *Feuilles mortes,* is a long, slow fade-out. *La Puerta del Vino* is yet another example of Debussy's genius at writing music about music. In it, he does not take his listeners to Spain, but rather filters its popular music through his own powerful imagination. In this piece he triumphantly captures the violence just below the surface of flamenco.

The elegant fourth prelude, *"Les fées sont d'exquises danseuses"* ("Fairies Are Exquisite Dancers"), cools things down wonderfully after the heat of *La Puerta del Vino*. Its long-spun phrases have a combination of delicacy and strength reminiscent of Mozart, although the music sounds only like Debussy. It opens with the same kind of billowing figuration as in *Brouillards,* here, moored firmly to the key of D-flat, deployed to utterly different effect. Debussy constantly alters melodies, phrase length, and rhythm to suggest the rapid movements of his sprite, from buzzing directly ahead to a more relaxed aerial ambling to hovering and sudden stops. But the choreographic grace of the music is unbroken, reaching a climax with a splendid, waltz-like passage marked to be played "caressingly." The beautiful figuration of the opening returns, and the work ends on three haunting notes, in which the pianist Paul Jacobs sensitively discerned an echo of Oberon's horn call from Carl Maria von Weber's fairy opera of the same name.

Bruyères (Heather) holds the calm center of Book II that was filled in Book I by *La fille aux cheveux de lin*, much as *La Puerta del Vino* fills its Spanish spot. This tranquil music strongly suggests an outdoor scene, evoking where the heather grows. It opens with a gentle melody that is reminiscent of that of *La fille aux cheveux de lin* but ranges just a bit more widely and moves more rapidly to remote harmonies. The middle section contains flutelike figuration, perhaps suggesting the presence of a shepherd, and a more intense melody, marked "joyous" by Debussy. He then brings the opening section back to end this sweet work in broad tranquility.

Général Lavine—excentric is a fantastical portrait of an American vaudevillian Debussy saw perform in Paris. The very tall entertainer dressed in a soldier's uniform to do his clowning. As in *Minstrels* of Book I, the music Debussy favors to create his portrait is the cakewalk, the jerky dance of the early jazz age. Again comes the harsh tootling of a trumpet in the opening, followed by the swagger of the cakewalk, ending in two comical bangs on a drum. Long, mock-awkward pauses, like the one that follows, form a crucial part of the texture of this prelude. The dance returns, amusingly if somewhat puzzlingly marked "spiritual and discreet" by the composer. The performer's pratfalls and other antics seem practically visible in the developments that follow. There is a moment of still seriousness right before a rather passionate outburst and the clattering ending. Although most of the musical elements of *Général Lavine* are herky-jerky and harsh on their own, Debussy's subtle employments of them, as well as the moments when he pulls back into stillness, make this a serious piece and a refined portrait.

The genesis of the beautiful, mysterious title *La terrasse des audiences du clair de lune* (The Terrace for Moonlight Audiences) for the great seventh prelude seems to be in an article recounting the coronation in 1912 of George V of England as emperor of India. Writer René Puaux poetically described "*la salle de la victoire, la salle du plaisir, le jardin des sultanes, la terrasse des audiences au clair de lune* . . .," which translates: "the hall of victory, the hall of pleasure, the garden of the sultanas, the terrace for moonlight audiences. . . ." Nothing more than this fine journalistic fragment stimulated Debussy's ready imagination to one of its highest peaks. His alteration of the word *au* (which means "in the") in the title to *du* ("of the") is incorrect, but no matter. The highly literate composer probably had his reasons for making the alteration, although they are unknown.

Musically as well as verbally, the work is saturated in mystery. Listeners seeking an Indian atmosphere will be disappointed, although one thematic element is suggestive of moonlight. But no tale takes place in the moonlight here, no sense at all that it is a narrative, a scene from nature, or a portrait—only beauty and deep feeling, set grandly but inscrutably. The allusive ambiguities of the meanings, spiritual profundity, and musical density of *La terrasse des audiences du clair de lune* place it a long way from the straightforward late romantic lyricism of *Clair de lune,* lovely as it is.

Only four minutes long but vast in scale, *La terrasse des audiences du clair de lune* opens with the ineffably dreamy motto that dominates it to the end. Almost immediately (0:05), a chromatic figure that could be associated with moonlight threads downward in the right hand. Another important four-note theme appears at 0:06 in the left. Note also at 0:05 the soft note deep in the bass that marks the first appearance of many, which, combined with high notes, form an important aspect of this prelude's voluptuous sonority. A rich chordal figure appears, beginning at 0:10, also marked by notes in the piano's deepest register at 0:11, 0:14, 0:22, and 0:28. The thready, moonlit figure recurs at 0:23 with the four-note theme below. At 0:32, the opening motto returns, gorgeously recast, trailed by a series of long, nearly motionless chords.

A new idea, faster-moving and more acrobatic, enters unexpected at 0:44. Running for 15 seconds only, it has no apparent connection with any of the other themes, nor does it reappear, yet Debussy fits it seamlessly into the flow of this magnificent musical stream. A crucial new melody appears (0:59), moving at the original pace, but with a more dancelike impulse. Debussy makes this quality more explicit at 1:13, as the figure moves with greater sinuous freedom, finally breaking out openly at 1:43 into a ghostly waltz with a decidedly Viennese lilt. But this waltz, too, presses urgently toward something greater.

The climax of the prelude, which begins at 1:56, is an awe-inspiring passage marked by massive chords played very softly high and low on the keyboard, after which the pianist must jump to the middle, then outward again. The great chords that follow starting at 2.10 mark the work's emotional climax; few listeners will be able to name the emotion they express, although their exaltation and ecstasy are absolutely clear. The unusual sonority of this tremendous passage has few peers: perhaps the closest can be heard in Beethoven's mystical late piano sonatas, in which notes sounded simultaneously at the far reaches of the instrument express a similar unearthly joy, to which few are privy but that the greatest artists can reveal.

From here (2:26), the work begins its long, majestic descent to the end. Graceful arpeggios leading into the waltz are heard at 2:41; the four-note theme recurs twice (2:51), followed by the descending moonlit figure at 2:59 and 3:04. Debussy slows the already broad pace to present the opening motto in a broken form (3:08), the floating chords, and a sinuous figure at 3:21. An astonishing passage with the distinct character of a processional begins at 3:26, followed by a big, glowing chord (3:39), as well as notes sounded high and deep to end this elusive but extraordinary work, which will never achieve the popularity of its more approachable companions.

Ondine, the eighth prelude, is the name of a mythological water sprite, stemming from the French word *onde,* or "wave." (The English word *undulate* has the same root.) This creature, a descendant perhaps of the Sirens of the *Odyssey* and certainly cousin to the Rhinemaidens of Wagner's *Ring,* is lovely but dangerous, luring men to their deaths with her beauty and the irresistibility of her song. Debussy's younger contemporary Ravel also composed an *Ondine* as the first movement of his great piano suite *Gaspard de la nuit,* for which title there is no adequate translation. The creature of Ravel's portrait seems genuinely dangerous, where Debussy's is more playful; both are certainly beautiful. In pianistic terms, the rippling figurations come directly from Liszt's wonderful depictions of water, from which both Frenchmen learned a great deal. This *Ondine* stands alongside *Jardins sous la pluie,* *L'isle joyeuse,* and *Poissons d'or* as one of Debussy's great aural depictions of moving water, from which only *Reflets dans l'eau* differs.

The prelude opens with a playful twitching figure that suggests the sprite's agile movements. Flowing scales and arpeggios (one marked "scintillating") follow, allowing listeners to see her moving through the water. A very beautiful dancelike theme appears, with a sunny tail given by Debussy the interesting expressive indication *"à l'aise"*—at ease. More developments of astonishing freshness and grace follow, powerfully suggesting the movement of light on and even in the water, as Debussy scatters individual repeated notes that seem like discrete droplets. The music starts and pauses frequently, like the fairies of *"Les fées sont d'exquises danseuses,"* but where their motion was airborne, this supple motion seems indisputably fluid. The work ends on a series of breathtakingly beautiful arpeggios. As with *Brouillards* and *"Les fées sont d'exquises danseuses,"* Debussy's rhythmic sense gives *Ondine* an enormous tensile strength beneath its glittering surface.

A relaxed, improvisatory tone pervades the wonderful *Hommage à S. Pickwick Esq. P.P.M.P.C.,* ninth in the set, making a fine and welcome contrast to the intensity of the two preceding pieces. As one might expect, Debussy had to employ considerable art in achieving its easy-going tone. The work opens with a humorously grandiose statement of "God Save the King," the British national anthem, in the left hand with broadly stated chords in the right. A gentle phrase (to be played "amiably," according to the composer's instructions) aptly limns Samuel Pickwick, the saintly old gentleman who is the hero of Dickens's first novel. More animated passagework follows, leading to an explosion of big chords, which may suggest his (not undeserved) self-esteem or his occasional fits of temper. More energetic passagework leads toward a shrill outburst that is cut off just before its climax, followed by an exquisite imitation of someone, perhaps Pickwick's devoted Cockney manservant Sam Weller, whistling a jig. This charming sketch, which is very much to the point and not nearly as loose-jointed as it sounds on first hearing, ends in the comically pompous tone in which it opened.

The mournful tenth prelude, *Canope,* once again contrasts strongly with what came before, as well as with what follows. This prelude,

short but evocative and profound, is named for the funerary jars first
discovered in the ancient Egyptian city of Canopus. Everything in this
intimate couple of minutes of music moves at a calm, sad, steady pace.
Eastern musical influences abound, and the work seems to drift away
rather than end. As Paul Roberts noted in *Images,*

> Debussy abandons the Western conception of harmonic progres-
> sion, of tension leading to resolution, and replaces it with, in
> his words, "the vibrant beauty of sound itself".... In *Canope,*
> resolution at the end is achieved not in the final chord, which in
> traditional terms remains unresolved, but after it, in the silence
> that follows the fading of the sounds. (164)

Alone among the preludes, the second to last, *Les tierces alternées*
(Alternating Thirds), is based on a purely musical idea. The characteristic sound of the common harmonic interval of the third rules
this trim work from start to finish. But Debussy extracts a variety of
sounds, touch, and even emotion that can hardly be anticipated by the
dry-sounding title. The work opens with slow thirds, after which a
series of quicker thirds appears, distributed evenly between the hands.
Melodic fragments emerge unexpectedly from the pattern, and the
composer employs an amazing range of combinations of the interval's
several forms to vary the sound and texture. The tempo slows, the key
changes, and, with a shift of the rhythm to a lilting dance, the middle
section, although still in thirds, presents a completely new face. The
opening section returns, bringing the work to a dryly funny ending.

As with *Voiles,* the title of the final prelude, *Feux d'artifice* (Fireworks;
track 12 on the compact disc) has two meanings: the first one, obvious
and outward, refers to the rocketry described so vividly by the music,
and the second suggests the fireworks of the music's showiness and
fearsome difficulty of execution. It is a display piece of considerable
dimension for the virtuoso pianist, perhaps the most difficult Debussy
composed. Liszt casts a major influence over this thrilling music, with
Debussy even echoing passages from one of that master's showpieces,
the Mephisto Waltz no. 1. The advanced harmonic scheme, in which
two keys are used at the same time, looks back at *Brouillards,* which
opens Book II. There are also similarities in how elaborate figuration

in one hand is set against chords in the other, although the radiant, fiery atmosphere of *Feux d'artifice* could hardly be more different from the eeriness and terror of that first prelude. It provides a stunning, magnificently satisfying conclusion to Book II, and to the entire series of twenty-four preludes.

The descriptive scenario is simple: *Feux d'artifice* presents the aural image of a Bastille Day fireworks display. Like any, the display is perceived far and near, growing in intensity to a tremendous climax, after which it ends nearly abruptly. It opens with a buzzing that could represent the hissing of fuses. A series of notes beginning at 0:05, starkly separated from one another, followed by a second series of softy struck, highly dissonant chords (0:13), hints at the first thrilling flashes of light from afar. At 0:23 the opening group is repeated at closer intervals, the volume jumps considerably (0:28), and with the tremendous slide known as a *glissando* at 0:34, it is easy to picture a falling rocket. At 0:40 a new, driving figure, strongly reminiscent of a theme from Liszt's Mephisto Waltz, is heard, like the skittering of another rocket. This figure moves upward toward a series of glowing scales beginning at 0:51, under which the climactic upward-reaching theme—not strictly a melody—makes its first, radiant appearance. This sharply accented motto is broken into three parts, at 0:56, 1:01, and, one second later, the final and wildest portion. The first portion recurs at 1:05 beneath dazzling figuration, then at 1:13 achieves a splashier incarnation—like a smoky pyrotechnic burst—above the roiling arpeggios. Another shower of pianistic sparks descends gloriously at 1:25.

At 1:31, Debussy finds another way to paint aurally how fireworks look in a new figure, not unlike the previous theme, but this delicate and dancelike. Softly played, it has the effect of fireworks viewed at some distance. A more intense iteration in jumpy, dissonant chords begins at 1:37, moving into another passage that picks up strongly on its choreographic hint and again refers to Liszt's Mephisto Waltz. At 1:56, a sharp note, marked "strident" by the composer, ends the aggressive waltz-like section, breaking into a new, softly played figure (2:03–2:09) that sounds the way cascading sparks look. An abrupt change of key marks a return of falling arpeggios, over and below which long, swaying melodies appear. Four massive but softly struck chords at 2:23, 2:26,

2:30, and 2:33 imitate with breathtaking accuracy the thud and glitter of larger explosions seen, heard, and felt from a distance. The arpeggios and sharply accented chords that lead to these allow the listener to "watch" the rockets' ascent before detonation.

Feux d'artifice now begins to move more urgently toward its climax, just as a good fireworks display keeps getting bigger and bolder. Arpeggios sweep ecstatically downward as the climactic thematic elements reappear, here in a new, more brusque rhythmic guise (2:39–2:44). At 2:47, an elaborate, sweeping passage known as a cadenza brings a new glitter to the music. At 3:01 the excitement mounts as Debussy presents the climactic theme in yet another, more breathless form, followed by another long cadenza, which builds furiously to broadly sweeping arpeggios over which the first portion of the main theme explodes, in its loudest, and therefore closest, incarnation (3:21). Now the display, stunning in its thunderous glory, seems to explode above our heads (3:40.) At 3:46, a shocking double arpeggio in two tonalities leads downward to the brief but remarkable closing section. Dimming flares lead to a grumbling in the keyboard's lower depths (3:54), and fragments of "La Marseillaise" are heard at 4:02 and 4:14 "from very far away," according to Debussy's instruction. Boldly, these are in a different key from the grumbling, accentuating the sense of distance from the listener, who by now feels like a viewer. The climactic fireworks motto makes final, faraway appearances at 4:07 and 4:19; this extraordinary creation ends on a bump in the bass.

The playful brilliance of *Feux d'artifice* contrasts with and actually highlights an immense power, and Debussy's use of two keys at once (known as bitonality), places him in the vanguard of twentieth-century music. His ability to build a potent, cohesive whole from fragmentary material is extraordinary, too. But what seems most remarkable about this final prelude is its expression of Debussy's genius for evoking spatial sensations near and far by tonal means. To accomplish this quality of nearness and distance, he uses notes that are high and low in addition to loud versus soft, as one expects. The result is profound as well as brilliant.

Pour le Piano IV:
The Late Works

ebussy's second book of preludes, completed in 1913, represents the final phase as well as the most lavish outpouring of
his psycho-pictorial style, as applied to the keyboard. They also
form a prelude in a different sense: they precede and lay the groundwork
for the few, exceptional final works Debussy composed for the piano.

The major works for piano comprise the twelve etudes and the
three-movement suite for two pianos, *En blanc et noir* (In Black and
White), and the *Six épigraphes antiques* for piano four hands. This brilliant music seems unlikely to achieve wide popularity, as the etudes are
wholly abstract, while the relatively uncommon two-piano and two-
pianist forms of *En blanc et noir* and the *Six épigraphes* form significant
obstacles to more frequent outings of these remarkable works.

Epigraphs are inscriptions, either on a tomb or monument, or the
pithy quotations at the start of a book or its chapters. Thus the *Six épigraphes antiques* of 1914 are as dense and quick as one might hope, with
the playing time for the entire set under fifteen minutes. Originally
written for two players at one instrument, Debussy later arranged them
for one pianist—to little effect, as they are rarely performed in either
version or in the effective orchestration by conductor Ernest Ansermet.
The rarity of the set's performance is a loss for players and audiences
alike, since there are few enough works from Debussy's pen in his late
period as it is. The *Six épigraphes* look back in countless ways on the
composer's earlier works, but with a completely fresh point of view.
Formally they seem somewhat loose in comparison with the earlier
piano works, but it is likely that in them Debussy simply dispensed
with transitional material, passing from one idea to the next without

ceremony, a common trait among great composers in their maturity. The effect of this structural freedom in the *Six épigraphes* is fresh and unbuttoned, not at all incongruous, reminiscent of Beethoven's late sets of Bagatelles (opp. 119 and 126). The keyboard textures most resemble those of the *Children's Corner*: light and open, unlike the dense textures of the *Estampes, Images,* preludes, or etudes.

The flood of references to earlier works can be nearly overwhelming when listening to the *Six épigraphes* of the first piece, *Pour invoquer Pan, dieu du vent d'été* (To Invoke Pan, God of the Summer Wind), the title alone evokes association with the Greek mythical conceptions of the *Prélude à l'après-midi d'un faune,* the *Danses sacrée et profane,* the *Syrinx* for solo flute, and the prelude *Danseuses de Delphes.* The musical echoes are there, as well. The main theme that relies on repeated tones recalls the preludes *La fille aux cheveux de lin* and *Bruyères,* but in the lilt of the quicker theme that follows there is something new. The opening of *Pour un tombeau sans nom* (For a Gravestone Without a Name) inevitably recalls that of *The Little Shepherd,* but the odd, five-beat time signature gives this work a strange, melancholy drift all its own. The next two works look forward with *Pour que la nuit soit propice* (That the Night May Be Auspicious, though for what the composer does not explain) recalls the insect sounds of *Ibéria's* central section and the infinitely detailed sound-world of *Jeux;* its insect noises inevitably call to mind Debussy's intense and brilliant successor Bartók. The following piece is *Pour la danseuse aux crotales* (For the Dancer with Crotales); crotales are castanets used by dancers in the theatrical rites of ancient Greece, the title inevitably linking this work with *Danseuses de Delphes. Pour la danseuse aux crotales* contains a passage that sounds as if it is lifted directly from a mid-twentieth-century bebop improvisation.

There is perhaps just a bit of hootchie-kootchie in the quasi-Asian flourishes of *Pour l'égyptienne* (For the Egyptian Woman), but the shifting, dusty harmonies over a syncopated bass of the middle section are atmospheric and utterly gorgeous. In the final, most beautifully titled *Épigraphe, Pour remercier la pluie au matin* (To Thank the Morning Rain), Debussy has crossbred some of his noblest works for the keyboard in this exquisite descendant. In this glorious study can be heard the repeated figuration of preludes that depict the sky in commotion,

Feux d'artifice and *Le vent dans la plaine,* into which are scattered melodic notes, in the manner of *Jardins sous la pluie.* But it is wrong to think of this as some sort of retread, just as it would be mistaken to look at Bach's *Art of the Fugue* or Chopin's late mazurkas as merely more of the same from their composers. The solemn but very fresh passage on which *Pour remercier la pluie* ends suggests the pantheist Debussy speaking to thank the rain for its cleansing. Any listener with a serious interest in the composer needs to hear these six mystically tinged expressions of his mature spirit.

Debussy dedicated the somber *Berceuse héroïque* (Heroic Lullaby) of 1914 to King Albert of Belgium, whose country had already suffered from the German invasion that followed the outbreak of World War I. It is impossible to hear in its funereal tread any emotions other than regret and sorrow. The faraway mock trumpet calls near the end contain only rue and no hint of pompous glory. Most likely it is this grimness, set forth more clearly here than in any of the master's compositions, that keeps it from performance; it is very rarely played or recorded, except in complete reviews of Debussy's piano music.

The onset of World War I depressed Debussy profoundly, shattering his concentration and productivity. As the German edition of Chopin's music was (like all publications from the enemy nation) banned in France, Debussy publisher Durand commissioned the composer to edit a new, French edition of the Polish master's work. Debussy's re-immersion into Chopin's music, which he already knew well and understood as profoundly as anyone, dazzled him with its power and beauty once again. In a burst of activity, he composed the twelve etudes in months, or perhaps even weeks, then dedicated them to Chopin's memory. (For a thorough though technical study of Chopin's profound and productive influence on Debussy, see Roy Howat's essay "Chopin's influence on the *fin de siècle* and beyond," in *The Cambridge Companion to Chopin,* edited by Jim Samson.)

Chopin composed two sets of twelve etudes, opp. 10 and 25, and a group of three, without opus number, called the *Trois Nouvelles Études.* These are artfully ordered for flow and contrast, but Chopin's sequence is not as tight as Debussy's. Debussy's dozen are broken into two groups of six, the first group covering types of fingering and musical intervals (the distances between notes) named numerically as thirds, fourths, sixths, and octaves, each with a characteristic sound and attendant problems in their musical expression. The second six are founded on more specifically pianistic matters, including grace notes, repeated notes, arpeggios, and fast-moving chords.

It seems unlikely that Debussy's etudes will ever achieve the popularity of Chopin's, or that of Debussy's own earlier piano works. They are abstract music, with no visual points of reference (although they do contain less specific tone painting), and Debussy's late, modernist harmonic idiom makes them tough going for many. But every one is a masterpiece, fully deserving the attention of serious listeners.

Written in the "plain" key of C major (the same key as Chopin's first etude) *Pour les "cinq doigts"—d'après Monsieur Czerny* (For the "Five Fingers"—after Mr. Czerny) affectionately parodies the exercises of Carl Czerny, still prescribed by thousands of piano teachers for their students. It is therefore first cousin to *Doctor Gradus ad Parnassum,* the opening piece of the *Children's Corner,* with which it shares a brightness of mood this inward composer rarely displays. The etude is, however, much more elaborate and difficult. Opening with a comically banal five-note scale into which an off-note intrudes, first quietly, then more insistently and off the beat. Sprays of skittish notes continue to interrupt the plain scales, finally breaking into a passage with the surging excitement that carries through to the very end. Notes splash freshly about, and the music reaches a thrashing climax, with Debussy throwing big chords, accompanied by racing arpeggios, over the keyboard. In a further display of good humor, Debussy marks the final, long scale to be played "noisily."

Like so much of Debussy's music, *Pour les "cinq doigts"* is referential and ironic, music about other music, in this case the basic scale studies with which all piano students wrestle. But it is imbued with unalloyed joy and excitement, a rushing, visceral pleasure that is uncommon for the often melancholy Debussy. When Debussy composed this music in 1915, he was suffering daily and directly from the cancer that would kill him three years later. But the first etude is an eruption of high spirits and wit; the writing of it must have done the composer good.

With *Pour les tierces* (For Thirds), Debussy returns to a more typically veiled emotional expression. The close interval of the third is notoriously difficult to negotiate, particularly in running passages, which is precisely what Debussy asks the pianist to do, just as Chopin did in his Etude in G-sharp minor, op. 25, no. 6. Keeping the running thirds chiefly in the right hand, Debussy milks the sound of the interval for its peculiar sweetness, looking back at Chopin's music all the while. One passage toward the end seems modeled on a similar theme in the first movement of Chopin's B minor sonata, op. 58. Yet here the harmony seems continually ready to float away in a manner Chopin—himself a fearless experimenter—could hardly have brought off, so vast were the changes in European music in the eighty years between the two composers' careers. This piece ends with an emphatic gesture of hammered chords. Apart from sharing the interval as a point of departure, *Pour les tierces* bears little resemblance to the prelude *Les tierces alternées*.

In a letter to his publisher, Debussy wrote of the third etude, *Pour les quartes* (For Fourths), "In it you will find some novel sonorities, although your ears are acclimatized to many an oddity" (qtd. in Schmitz 200). Debussy's offhand remark hits the nail on the head: despite the near-century of music that has followed, *Pour les quartes* remains one of his most daring conceptions, still unsettling to hear. Its boldness stems from the use of the fourth, a dissonant interval in classical harmony, as its building block. The floating feel of the fourth lends the piece its peculiar ability to disturb, as well as its beauty. It is not only the eerie, delicate harmony that is unusual, however, but the ever-shifting tempo and keyboard color, as well. The pianist constantly moves from gently played notes to passages that are hammered; Debussy's expressive markings are wide-ranging but specific, instructing the player to perform "danceably and gracefully," "playfully," "calmly," "with sadness," "faraway," "more slowly and dying away," "effortlessly flowing," and, for the final chord, *"estinto"*—for which "extinguished" is perhaps the best translation. This profound work is not only a landmark of modern music, showing influence particularly on Bartók, who favored the fourth in his works, but one of the purest examples of Debussy's ability to enchant—and disturb—through sound alone, without recourse to traditional processes of thematic development.

The sweet sound of the sixth is the technical basis of the fourth etude, *Pour les sixtes.* Chopin's spirit hovers above this work, as well, in which Debussy pays playful tribute to his predecessor's love of Italian operatic melody and his flexible approach to piano sonority. The mellifluous sonority of the sixth also dominates two of Chopin's important compositions, the Etude in D-flat major, op 25, no. 8, and the Nocturne, op. 27, no. 2, in the same key. Debussy's approach to a D-flat etude in sixths differs from Chopin's, in that Debussy's is gentle, where the earlier composer's is fast and athletic. As in *Pour les quartes,* changes of tempo form a significant part of this etude's expressive posture, with almost constant hesitations and accelerations making the pianist's job more difficult. *Pour les sixtes* fades languorously away in a long, dying fall worthy of Chopin, the master of such passages.

The glittering octave, as hammered out by countless piano virtuosi in too many works to mention, is the basis of *Pour les octaves.* Debussy takes advantage of the octave's aggressive personality to change the pace and tone from the quieter, more restrained expression of the last three etudes to one of athletic exuberance and joy. *Pour les octaves* is a breathtaking waltz of grand sweep and immense difficulty. The broad flow of the opening section gives way to the steadier rhythm of the middle section and the pointillism of its detached notes. These sprayed and rapid-fire notes lead to a passage with the remarkable expressive instruction "with a muffled turbulence," then the same passage in a different key marked "noisily." A quieter section leads to a fiery close, a cathartic moment in any complete performance of the etudes. While this exuberant, very French waltz sounds little like Chopin's fourteen soulful essays in the form, Debussy's (like Chopin's) is about the dance, and emphatically not for dancing.

Debussy devised the witty sixth etude, *Pour les huit doigts* (For Eight Fingers) as a comic counterpoise of the first study. His footnote at the bottom of the opening page of this piece reads: "In this etude the changing positions of the hands makes the use of the thumbs uncomfortable, and its execution with them becomes acrobatic." From the beginning, pianists have taken this note as a challenge to find ways to use their thumbs, at which task many have succeeded, the first being Marguerite Long. Applauding her spunk, Debussy immediately authorized the use of thumbs (Roberts 310). So the furiously buzzing notes of this difficult-sounding piece may be somewhat easier in execution than they appear. In this work, tight patterns, chiefly of four notes but sometimes of two, dominate. Debussy slips a melody in underneath the steady, insect-like buzz; there is a huge slide, preceding a return of the dizzy whir. Again, a melody rises from under the activity in the left hand, and, following a couple of hectic falling scales, the etude ends comically on two bare G-flats, five wide and empty octaves apart.

The second group of six opens with a work that draws on the first and sixth etudes. Like those, *Pour les degrés chromatiques* (For Chromatic Notes) is a whirling finger study, and it draws slithery, slippery sound from Debussy's continual use of the black keys. This etude opens with a splash of frisky octaves above fast notes, its playful nature immediately evident. A melody with a strong rhythmic profile enters in the left hand, but rapidly shifting harmony leaves the listener filled with uncertainly as to where the melody and harmony are headed. The pace of *Pour les degrés chromatiques* is so quick, however, that one hardly has time to wonder before the work spins itself out, like a top.

The title of the eighth etude, *Pour les agréments,* is sometimes translated as "For Ornaments," with the noun occasionally rendered as "embellishments." Debussy described this great work, the last of the etudes to be written, as "a barcarolle, on a somewhat Italian sea" (Schmitz 209), inevitably reminding listeners of Chopin's singular masterpiece (op. 60), which, according to students, Debussy adored and taught brilliantly (Samson 257, 326n). Debussy's "barcarolle" bears some resemblance to Chopin's, although the ornaments he employs so abundantly derive more from the vocal and keyboard music of the French masters of the baroque era than from Chopin's Italian vocal models. *Pour les agréments* shares with Chopin's *Barcarolle* a gentle but pervasive rocking motion, above which Debussy creates profuse rhythmic variations, as well as a lavish pianistic texture and a wealth of thematic elements, perhaps the most memorable being a long, celestial melody with a strange, mincing gait, first heard in the right hand, then reinterpreted in the bass. And yet for the all the richness of *Pour les agréments,* its lambent purity and bottomless depth make it one of Debussy's most astonishing compositions.

The ninth etude, *Pour les notes répetées* (For Repeated Notes), is another fast and playful interlude. Resembling in form a toccata, a virtuosic piece with an improvisatory character from the baroque era, *Pour les notes répetées* is in three sections. The jerky rhythms of the outer sections lend the music a grotesque character reminiscent of *Golliwogg's Cake-walk* and *Minstrels,* Debussy's earlier pieces drawing on the dances of Black American musical reviews. As pianist Paul Roberts points out in *Images,* his loving study of Debussy's keyboard works (312), its rapid-fire notes are also close in spirit to Liszt's etude *La campanella,* an inspired transcription of one of Paganini's caprices for violin. The easing of tempo in the brief central section provides a sense of relaxation, though in fact the fast notes continue throughout.

Stravinsky's much-repeated description of Beethoven's *Grosse Fuge* as "contemporary forever" applies just as well to Debussy's tenth piano etude, *Pour les sonorités opposées* (For Contrasting Sonorities). The neutral title gives little sense of the scope of this sublime summation of Debussy's experience as a composer for the piano. The opening notes, widely spaced and utterly daring in harmony, precede a long, sweeping melody indeed "expressive and profound," as the composer marked it, followed by a doleful passage that moves with slow, steady gravity over the keyboard, its chords stuck high and low to unforgettable effect. Following this, a "distant, but clear and joyous," passage, recalling the spatial effects of the preludes *"Et les sons . . ."* from Book I and the *Feux d'artifice* (track 12), sounds in the right hand. The sweeping melody is reiterated with tragic exaltation, then sinks downward; the long, complex closing passage invokes Chopin in its elaborate sprays of grace notes and pure piano sound; the distant figure recurs several times before disintegrating, leading to the rising rich broken chords that conclude the piece.

Pour les sonorités opposées is the spiritual climax of the etudes and one of the pinnacles of the piano literature. The "opposing sonorities" of the reticent title refers to the infinitely wide range of touch, from dense, thundering chords to the most delicate tracery that the performing artist must deploy. But the demands imposed on the interpretive powers and concentration of the pianist and his or her audience are greater yet.

The graceful eleventh etude provides relief to the nervous system and is said to be one of the easier to play, as well. For these reasons, *Pour les arpèges composés* (For Combined Arpeggios) was long the most popular member of this difficult set. A beautiful tune emerges from the long-limbed arpeggios of the opening, after which more rapid and athletic passages sweep the keyboard; yet there is ecstasy in this music, as well, with one especially brilliant arpeggio marked to be played "luminously." The central section, with its strumming texture, is a more playful interlude in Debussy's Spanish mode, and the final sweeps up and down the keyboard toward the exquisite close are warm and genuinely touching. Reminiscent of the prelude *Ondine* in its relaxed and elegant lyricism, *Pour les arpèges composés* provides a few moments of repose between the intensity of *Pour les sonorités opposées* and the terrors of the final etude.

Gooseflesh can be expected when a pianist of great physical strength tears into the opening passage of the last etude, *Pour les accords* (For Chords). The muscular chords are placed widely over the keyboard, requiring tremendous precision, as well as speed. But it is their relentless, biting fury that grabs the nervous system with such power. The frequent shifts of rhythmic emphasis add difficulty for the player, while further unsettling the listener. Nor does the remote brooding of the icy central section provide relief. The "sweet, flowery, flowing" Debussy beloved by the uninitiated is nowhere to be found in this snarling music, nor the triumphant, pantheistic tone poet of *La mer*. Instead, the composer here sets forth, in tightly organized phrases, a fearsome vision of violence and nihilism.

Pour les accords is also a pivotal work in the history of piano music, looking backward to the virtuoso etudes of Chopin and Liszt, and ahead to the works of Stravinsky, Bartók, Hindemith, and Boulez, who would treat the piano as a percussion instrument. In general, Debussy's etudes hold a singular position in the piano literature, from the energetic parody of Czerny in *Pour les "cinq doigts,"* to the savage rhythms of *Pour les accords*. Looking back to Rameau, Couperin, and Liszt, and bravely forward, Debussy even reviews his own earlier contributions to the literature for the keyboard; with Chopin's glorious achievement hovering above all. Their difficulty as music must not discourage listeners from hearing the etudes often.

Debussy composed the two-piano suite *En blanc et noir* (In Black and White) in 1915, a crucial element of his final, remarkable creative outburst. A staple of the slim, generally lightweight two-piano repertoire, *En blanc et noir* is a work of striking power and passion, while displaying the desperate beauty that is the hallmark of the composer's late style; it is also highly advanced musically. Originally titled *Caprices en blanc et noir,* the composer removed the first word from the manuscript he sent to his publisher; the plainer title, with its moving evocation of the keyboard, seems better suited to the density and power of the score.

Each of the three movements has a separate dedication and an epigraph—precisely the kind of short quotation used to set the mood referred to in the title of the *Six épigraphes antiques.* At the practical level, it would be ridiculous for two pianists to learn and perform just one or two of the three movements. But even though the individual dedications and epigraphs seem to hint that the movements are independent, like those of the *Estampes* or *Images,* and there is no obvious musical connection among the three movements, *En blanc et noir* is surely, if perhaps indefinably, a unified aesthetic whole.

The opening movement, dedicated to the Russian conductor Serge Koussevitzky (1874–1951), begins with a sweeping phrase that hurtles ahead breathlessly. Debussy's expression marking is *"avec emportement"*—with transport—and there is no mistaking the passion in this music, expressed with a catch-in-the-throat directness that is uncommon for the composer. The movement consists of a procession of fantastical ideas, presented mostly at breakneck speed: a fanfare, a broad, rocking melody, and a sequence of individual notes that sound spat out. A passage involving much hand crossing for the second pianist leads into a sequence of raging mock military trumpet calls (*En blanc et noir* is drenched in sound images of war) that move quickly into a jazzy bass rhythm that runs far ahead of its date or cultural milieu. The opening melody returns, leading into a headlong, wildly passionate closing page that is, like the entire movement, as moving as anything Debussy composed.

The second movement, longest by far of the three, is the most directly expressive of the composer's grief and patriotism over the war. Dedicated to *"Lieutenant Jacques Charlot tué à l'ennemi en 1915, le 3 Mars"*—killed by the enemy on March 3, 1915—Debussy's initial marking of tempo and expression is "Slow. Somber." The terrible chords that open the movement speak of its character. Another mock trumpet call enters, played by the first pianist, then two more melodies with folk-like accents. A series of repeated chords expresses Debussy's deepest sorrow and mystical rapture. A new idea enters at a faster tempo that expresses trouble and conflict, developing into a furious, driving bass, followed by a new melody above, the famous Lutheran chorale *Ein feste Burg ist unser Gott* (A Mighty Fortress Is Our God), representing the imperialist Germany Debussy loathed. There is an astonishing musical struggle between the German chorale and folk melodies, backed by the mock trumpet call; an ecstatic passage of brightly hammered Stravinskian chords for the first piano is accompanied by a breathless, almost giddy statement of the trumpet call for the second, but this victory is only in notes—in black and white—as Debussy himself knows all too well. Both pianos render a distorted phrase from "La Marseillaise" in steady, chiming notes. The initial tempo returns, again in solemn chords that have a different tone after what they have endured, as the composer guides this remarkable movement to an agonized, gripping conclusion. In this astonishing passage, Debussy creates a powerful, twisting iteration of the trumpet call and chords that state the sharp rhythm of its stunning battle cry *"Aux armes!"*—To arms!—from Rouget de Lisle's iconic anthem. But Debussy's harmony is dark and the notes move down, giving the phrase the feel of a prophetic and terrible warning to his countrymen. This tremendous piece makes harrowing listening.

The third movement is dedicated to *"mon ami Igor Stravinsky."* The influence of Debussy's young friend can be heard in the rhythmic fluidity of this choreographic music, as well as in its near atonality, which Stravinsky himself pointed out, according to the pianist Paul Jacobs, in notes about *En blanc et noir* for his own performance of the work with Gilbert Kalish. Although lighter in texture and mood than its companions, its sardonic posture and frequent shifts of tempo and tone make it other than relaxing listening. Landmarks include a folk-like melody that never quite finishes and a vehemently hammered figure for both left hands. Quiet, icy chords over a grumbling bass, followed by four slithering arpeggios for the first piano, lead to the casually spooky end. *En blanc et noir* stands out even in the rich harvest of greatness in Debussy's post-1913 oeuvre.

The Songs

T he French art-song tradition was fairly well established when in the mid-1870s the teenaged Debussy began setting poetic texts to music. Jules Massenet (1842–1912), most famous as an operatic composer, also composed about two hundred songs; Gabriel Fauré (1845–1924) composed dozens over the course of his long career, including many of great beauty (his setting of Verlaine's poem *Clair de lune* is lovely, surpassing Debussy's youthful song, which has nothing to do with the famous piano work from *Suite bergamasque*). The tale of Henri Duparc (1848–1933) is one of the saddest in musical history. Before illness silenced his magnificent gift at age thirty-six, Duparc composed the sixteen glorious songs that are a staple of the vocal repertory. And there is *Nuits d'été* (Summer Nights), the extraordinary song cycle with orchestra by Hector Berlioz (1803–1869). Although Berlioz is one of the genuine eccentrics in musical history, these six extraordinary songs speak to the heart and mind with a clarity not always found in the composer's work, but with Berlioz's vivid imagination fully engaged, as well. Maurice Ravel (1875–1937) and Francis Poulenc (1899–1963) are the two greatest practitioners of the art song in France after Debussy. Both composed dozens of wonderful songs that entered the standard repertory with ease; these are, on the whole, easier to approach then Debussy's.

The intimate and restrained vocal style of *Pelléas et Mélisande* gives a good sense of Debussy's songs: like the opera, they are meticulously wrought works very much in their own class. The composer wrote more than eighty songs over the course of his career, most before the turn of the century; the earliest, of which *Beau soir* (Lovely Evening;

track 13 on the enclosed compact disc), composed by Debussy at around sixteen, are straightforward lyrical outpourings that may be derivative of Massenet and others but that are irresistible nonetheless.

A free translation of Paul Bourget's text is: "When the sun sets, the rivers are pink, and a warm wave runs across the fields of wheat, happy tidings seem to rise toward the troubled heart, a taste of the world's charms—as long as one is young and the evening is beautiful. But we are going, like that wave, it to the sea, we to the grave."

Debussy's matches Bourget's simple lyric with a musical simplicity, with the shifting harmonies of the arpeggios (0:01–0:15) that open the work suggesting not just the rippling wheat and the beauty of the evening, but the fatalistic twist of the final line. The singer's "happy tidings" are matched by a change in texture, away from the sweeping broken chords to a gently rocking figure over solid chords (0:40) and a shift to the major. The climax comes on the words "and the evening is beautiful" (1:15). Debussy shifts down easily, leaving the singer the phrase "it to the sea" (1:39) without accompaniment, perhaps anticipating his mature aesthetic of refusing to allow musical accompaniment to drown words. The opening chords, now full of meaning, are set against the final phrase (1:47 to the end).

Although *Beau soir* is the earliest and by far the simplest work on the CD, one must admire the adolescent composer's skill at expressing a young man's painful awareness of the beauty and evanescence of life. More significant, though, is his remarkable sensitivity to the text, a quality that would only grow as he matured. Debussy needed to be interested in the texts he set, as the subsequent sets of songs would show. Again and again, he set poems by Verlaine, Mallarmé, and Baudelaire, perhaps the three most important French poets of the late nineteenth and early twentieth centuries. He also set to music those of the fifteenth-century poets François Villon and Charles d'Orléans, the sixteenth-century poet Tristan Lhermite, the work of his friend Pierre Louÿs, and his own texts.

Among the earlier works there are other charming examples, but it is only with the ambitious *Cinq poèmes de Baudelaire* of 1889 that strong hints of the mature Debussy may be heard. The sliding chromatic scales of *C'est l'extase* (It Is Ecstasy), the opening song of *Ariettes oubliées* (Forgotten Ariettas), composed in 1888 to poems by Verlaine, frankly portrays postcoital languor. With the *Fêtes galantes* (difficult to translate, but "Gallants' Parties" will have to do) of 1891, Debussy's growing skill and point of view are clearer yet, with *Fantoches* (Puppets) a memorable piece. Debussy set the four *Proses lyriques* of 1893 to his own texts, which seem overloaded with their burden of imagery. But the music is very beautiful and unmistakably the work of a mind freeing itself from constraints; no surprise, as these are from the same period as the *Prélude à l'après-midi d'un faune* and the String Quartet. The floating harmony of the opening of *De rêve* (Dream), first song in the set, shows the vast distance the young composer had traveled from the conventions of the parallel passage of *Beau soir*.

Debussy's friend Pierre Louÿs wrote the texts for the three *Chansons de Bilitis* (Songs of Bilitis, the last word being a woman's name) of 1897, saying he had translated them from previously unpublished poems from ancient Greece. The minor scandal that blew up when the facts came out is nearly forgotten. The poems are deeply sensual in character, and Debussy's extraordinarily sensitive settings rank them among his masterpieces. These evocations of a long-lost world (more accurately, one that never existed) also stand proudly among the composer's other "Greek" works: the *Prélude à l'après-midi d'un faune,* the *Danses sacrée et profane,* and above all, the prelude *Danseuses de Delphes.*

In 1904 Debussy set a second trio of poems by Verlaine, also under the title of *Fêtes galantes*. *Le faune* (The Faun), second of these, is interesting not least for the imaginative evocation by the piano of drums and flutes. Also from 1904 are the two rondels, a medieval form, by Charles d'Orléans, an interesting figure who was a prince in France's royal family. These are notable for a deliberately archaic tone and posture, creating a sophisticated faux recollection of the harshly beautiful music of the time. *Le promenoir des deux amants* (The Walk of the Two Lovers) consists of two sad poems and one love song by Tristan Lhermite. The first, *Auprès de cette grotte sombre* (Beside This Dark Cave), is an icy musical landscape that clearly and movingly anticipates the desolate piano prelude *Des pas sur la neige,* from Book I. The second, *Crois mon conseil, chère Climène* (Take My Advice, Dear Climène), is a free musical rendering of Lhermite's high classical text, executed with the greatest delicacy. *Je tremble en voyant ton visage* (I Tremble When Seeing Your Face) echoes some of the master's great piano music of the early years of the century, notably *Pagodes*. Debussy worked on this triptych of reticent masterworks from 1904 to 1910, dedicating them to Chouchou.

The three *Ballades de François Villon* (1910) are stark settings of three longish poems by the well-known fifteenth-century poet and criminal. The first song is a bitter complaint to the poet's false lover; the second a prayer to the Virgin. Third, and surely most entertaining, is the *Ballade des femmes de Paris* (Ballad of the Women of Paris), which humorously compares the women of different cities and states (Florence, Venice, Naples, Greece, England, and many others) to those of Paris, with the Parisians of course winning the poet's judgment. Debussy imposed on all three settings, as with those of the Charles d'Orléans poems, a deliberate coarseness, to suggest the hard-edged secular music of 450 years earlier.

The composer's final triptych of song settings are of works by Stéphane Mallarmé, Debussy's friend and poet of *L'après-midi d'un faune*. Composed in 1913, these display all the sophisticated technique one might expect, notably in their austere, condensed harmonic schemes and lack of big musical gestures. These intimate works are surely jewels, but not for the common ear. The song *Noël des enfants qui n'ont plus de maison* (Christmas for Children Who Have Lost Their Homes) is a powerful wartime document of 1915. Debussy himself wrote the angry text, in which children who have lost homes and parents pray for vengeance for themselves and the "little Belgians, Serbs, and Polish, too!" This potent text is set to an accompaniment that shudders with rage and despair.

Although Debussy's songs form a part of his oeuvre that is important and of the highest quality, they have never had broad popularity and probably never will. There are many reasons for this lack of wide appeal: first, vocal music has long lagged far behind instrumental in popularity with American audiences. And the art song has perhaps the smallest audience of any form of classical music, though it is one of the most fanatical. The songs demand unusual concentration from performer and listener alike, with each a precious vehicle of words, vocal line, and accompaniment. Debussy's songs share all the subtlety and polish of his other works; they are also, according to singers, difficult to put across. Thus, while they contain music that stands with the composer's best, their compact, refined form and content remain inaccessible to the casual listener. Even the interested music lover must go more than halfway to meet the demands of Debussy's songs, setting aside a quiet hour to listen without distraction to this exceedingly subtle music, which simply cannot be appreciated while cooking dinner or driving.

The Chamber Works

All four of Debussy's major pieces for chamber ensembles—the String Quartet of his early maturity and three very late sonatas—are of a high order. But the three other works of lesser dimension, nearly equal in quality to the big pieces, are also well worth knowing. Fortunately, the several fine recordings of Debussy's complete chamber works on the market make it easy for the interested listener to hear the entire group. The delicious *Rapsodie* for clarinet and piano, written in 1910 as a competition piece for students at the Paris Conservatory, is the same one orchestrated by the composer in the following year, but somehow the more intimate original version seems more pleasing. The *Petite pièce* for clarinet and piano, also dating to 1910, was devised as a sight-reading test; it, too, is a lovely morsel by the mature master, if anything too short at under two minutes' playing time.

The *Syrinx* for solo flute is even more remarkable. Conceived by Debussy in 1913 as incidental music for the play *Psyché,* by Gabriel Mourey, this astonishing three minutes of music for solo flute stands as one the purest example of the composer's aesthetic. Only breath through a metal tube, *Syrinx* is purest line, sound, and mood, hovering on the brink of existence. This magical evocation of Pan's death song is also a moving descendant of the *Prélude à l'après-midi d'un faune* of two decades earlier. *Syrinx* is Debussy's art at its most paradoxical, at once exquisitely refined and potent. *Density 21.5* of 1936 for solo flute by the experimentalist Edgard Varèse (1883–1965) is unimaginable without *Syrinx* as its forerunner.

Debussy completed the String Quartet no. 1 in G minor, op. 10, in the summer or autumn of 1893; it was premiered by the Ysaÿe Quartet on 29 December of that year. The String Quartet no. 1 holds a singular position in Debussy's oeuvre: it is his only work in this revered form, despite the sequence implied by its numbered title, and his only work with an opus number. But the exceptional position of the quartet in the composer's output goes far deeper than mere numerical quirks: of all Debussy's works, it is probably the most rigorously classical in form and is something of an oddity within the output of this brave seeker after individual, internally generated structures for virtually everything else he composed.

Carried to dizzying heights by Haydn, Mozart, and Beethoven, the string quartet is the intellectual crown of classical instrumental forms. These masters found in the little ensemble of two violins, viola, and cello the means to express ideas that stand among their most profound, and for Haydn and Beethoven, their most daring, as well. Their string quartets rely heavily on the conflicts inherent in sonata process, which Debussy avoided. And so, here, in his only quartet, the composer employs cyclical form, in which the main theme recurs repeatedly over the course of the work, with that opening theme—the work's "motto"—returning to end the piece in the fourth movement, a technique pioneered by Beethoven, Liszt, and Berlioz, and taken to another level by the Belgian composer César Franck (1822–1890). The themes of Debussy's quartet move sequentially, none doing battle with another, but the work has a linear austerity not evident elsewhere in his output.

The quartet's first movement opens directly with a statement, for all four instruments, of the opening theme, muscular and urgent, clothed in a droning harmony. The throbbing rhythmic device known as a *triplet* forms a crucial element of this powerful tune, as it will in all the movements of the quartet. A long, sighing melody that is an extension and subtle variant of the main motto, taking the place of a second theme, appears, passing from violin to cello over a rippling accompaniment; but the opening melody returns quietly, in rapidly shifting harmonic incarnations. Another long tune enters without ceremony, leading to a climactic passage, after which another theme, the true, thoughtfully

lyrical second subject enters, also ripe with triplets, followed by a forceful, angular statement of the opening. There is, however, no development section in the traditional sense: at no time does Debussy pull his
melodies apart or pit them against one another in conflict; he simply
runs them in a single, artful, driving sequence. The thoughtful theme
does provide the movement's more relaxed moments, which ends on a
powerful rhythmic variation of the opening.

The breathtaking second movement relies on the sound of the
plucked (pizzicato) strings for its characteristic sound, as well as on
a complex but agile rhythmic structure of the kind Debussy would
use again in the *Rondes de printemps,* third of the orchestral *Images.*
Everything in the movement's tight structure is relevant to the motto
theme, which here also serves as the chief melody, though transformed
in rhythm and personality. Even the violin melody that floats over
the rippling bowed strings of the middle section is the motto tune,
stretched out and made a bit difficult to recognize. The cello's massive, guitar-like plucked chords anticipate those of the late Cello Sonata
(tracks 14 through 16), although that work has a Spanish accent that
is less pronounced here. The sound of this fantastical music, utterly
refreshing from beginning to its elegant end, clearly inspired the parallel movement of Ravel's only string quartet, also built on the pizzicato
sonority.

Some listeners, including Debussy's English biographer Edward
Lockspeiser, hear in the pensive third movement the quartet's emotional climax (169). In the opening sequence, the main theme of
the movement, which is not the motto but rises and falls like it, is
interspersed with grave chords. Certainly, the passionate passage
Lockspeiser quotes (into which a triplet is woven) is also more personal
than any other utterance in the work. Debussy brings the movement to
a close on a rueful reiteration of the main melody, which he marks to
be played in a "weakening" tone, and a last, high, solemn chord, tinged
with sweetness.

The finale has the tightest and most elaborate structure of all, with
Debussy performing in it his single overt imitation of and obeisance
to Beethoven. As is the finale of the Ninth Symphony, themes from
the earlier movements are restated, though not gruffly rejected, as in

Beethoven. A contrapuntal passage—exceedingly rare for Debussy—built on the motto theme leads to an angry climax and a falling sequence for all four instruments that ends in muttering for the cello. From this grumbling, the main theme emerges, a grim and aggressive variant of the motto, first stated by the viola. But more lyrical elements soon enter, and the composer's characteristic grace and rhythmic flexibility are also amply displayed. Eventually, the main theme of the first movement returns in a major key and with high energy; the work ends on a statement of the motto that is exciting and powerful but without a hint of Germanic pomp.

The String Quartet is an unqualified masterwork, firmly enthroned among the elite repertory of this lofty and competitive category of instrumental music. Debussy's labors are particularly admirable for the deftness with which he maintains a French mobility and lightness of sound and texture in so abstract and serious a form, and for the clarity with which his compositional voice comes through. But the experiment was not one the composer chose to repeat. Instead, he looked elsewhere to find inspiration for his final trio of masterworks for chamber ensembles.

The final three chamber sonatas were all Debussy managed to complete of a group of six he proposed in 1914 to his publisher, Durand. These he began in the heroic burst of energy that also produced the etudes for piano and *En blanc et noir*; however, for a variety of reasons, chiefly deteriorating health, he struggled to complete them. Besides the three finished sonatas, Debussy planned to compose a fourth for oboe, horn, and harpsichord but died before tackling this work as well as the projected but unnamed fifth and sixth of the series. The finished works represent the composer's style at its most modern and condensed, although the Violin Sonata—his final work—is considered by many critics to be weaker than its companions. Yet in all three, the dying Debussy seems to speak from another plane. In a show of wartime patriotism, Debussy took pains to describe himself on their title page as a *"musicien français."*

Debussy completed the Sonata for Cello and Piano, a landmark in its small but distinguished repertory, in 1915. It has never achieved wide popularity, a fact that, given its strange, highly personal utterance, is hardly surprising. The fearless, big-boned performance on the CD at the back of the book by pianist Martha Argerich and cellist Mischa Maisky grabs the listener in a way not all recordings of the Cello Sonata achieve. (Performances that treat Debussy with kid gloves—as this one emphatically does not—have for a century misled listeners as to the true, vibrant nature of his music.) It is helpful to remember when listening to this deeply original music that it is ironic in tone from beginning to end and that it moves through a kaleidoscopic range of moods, of which some are playful but few are particularly happy. Also, the neutral title betrays nothing about the Spanish character of the music, which is as intense here as in *Ibéria, La Puerta del Vino,* or *Soirée dans Grenade,* at times surpassing them in an exoticism that is positively Moorish.

The structure of the Cello Sonata is organic, imposed by the ebb and flow of musical ideas and emotions rather than by any standard format, as such structures were nearly irrelevant to Debussy late in his career. The composer carries thematic cells, particularly four-note turns, freely within and between the first and third movements, while the second movement, *Sérénade,* has an acidly comic scenario of its own. Finally, while Debussy uses both instruments in unusual ways here, the sounds he gets from the cello are particularly daring. The rich, baritonal singing for the cello heard in music for the instrument by Beethoven, Mendelssohn, Chopin, Schumann, Brahms, and Dvorak is far less in evidence, replaced by other sounds—especially a remarkable variety of plucked strings, as well as bowing on the fingerboard—that produce a gritty sonority that looks far ahead to work by composers of later generations, including Xenakis, Maderna, and Boulez.

The opening movement, titled *Prologue,* begins with a proclamation for the piano, of which swaggering triplets (0:02 and 0:10) form an important element. The cello enters with a rising arpeggio (0:14) in the same spirit as the piano; the Spanishness of the tone is impossible to mistake. The piano drops out for a moment, the cello continuing with a moody soliloquy (0:20) built of roulades and flourishes. The key melody enters at 0:45, a sad, falling tune in broken phrases over simple chords for the piano, then repeated, beginning at 1:06, over piano chords in more remote harmony. At 1:33, another cello melody in faster notes enters, sounding like the half-spoken, half-sung wail of the *cante jondo* imitated so tellingly in the piano works *La Puerta del Vino* and *Soirée dans Grenade*. Debussy uses this rhythm as a transition to the next idea (1:57), fast and fantastical, which moves with choreographic grace and fluidity; at 2:08 the piano's even accompaniment changes to spectral chords, creating a surprising approach to the return of the opening flourish, stated powerfully by the cello (2:20). Another brooding episode follows, marked by arabesques (2:28), as the tempo slows and Debussy introduces a new, rising figure for the cello in triplet rhythm (2:56) that, however, feels bereft of energy. The cello delicately plays a series of passionate flourishes over a snapped piano chord, but this series fades away.

The closing section of the movement is artfully constructed of recollections of earlier material, in ever-thinning textures and tempos that slow gradually, leading to a return of the sad main melody at 3:20, repeated more slowly at 3:43. The triplets come back, here grave and sorrowful (3:59, 4:15, and 4:21), as the cello line drifts upward with smoky, weightless grace to a final chord played in harmonics (4:42), a technique in which the cellist touches the strings lightly to produce a glassy tone. A final bump in the piano ends the movement.

Debussy offers no hint as to who is performing the parodistic *Sérénade* that is the short second movement, or for whom it is performed, but this is a study of peculiar sonorities, remarkable as well as for its musical density, dizzying mood changes, and comic brittleness. The *Sérénade* opens with the unusual sound of the cello playing a rising figure in pizzicato, to which the piano replies in kind. The cello's notes pull upward (0:04–0:07), sounding like a guitar that is being tuned, and both cello and piano spend most of the movement imitating the guitar. The main melody, a stiff, old-fashioned kind of serenade rendered in weird harmony, enters at 0:15 in pizzicato notes interspersed with bowed ones (0:25 and 0:29). At 0:40, a solitary note, plucked hard, suggests a less-than-skilled guitarist, a broken string, or perhaps a cheap, recalcitrant instrument. Another, longer phrase of the serenade enters (0:44), marked, however, to be played "ironically." The melody continues; on the long sliding cello note at 0:54 one can hear the singer's drooping voice. But again (1:01) the guitar seems to have fallen out of tune and requires attention.

The serenade resumes again at 1:10, continuing with various accelerations, slowdowns, and shifts between plucking and bowing for the cellist, although the pizzicato dominates. At 1:40, strummed chords for the piano show that it has become the guitar, while the cello has taken on the vocal role in this little wrestling match between the irritated serenader and his instrument. A series of roulades beginning at 1:43 continues the Moorish vein of the opening movement, finally landing in another comic episode in which the piano plays in a false rhythm (1:50) that quickly smooths out. The longest and most beautiful snatch of song begins (2:08), with the cello imitating a falsetto at 2:22. But the comically frustrated serenader never really gets going. Again, brusque pizzicati interrupt the melodic flow at 2:29, 2:39, and 2:47.

Once again, the guitarist must try to tune up (2:54), then resumes his song at 3:06. The cello takes the vocal line once more, while the piano plays the chords, strummed and plucked, of the guitar (3:15, 3:21, and to the end).

The idea of an interrupted Spanish serenade fascinated Debussy. The little violin solo shouldered aside by the orchestral mass in the last part of *Ibéria* is one instance; the piano prelude *La sérénade interrompue* from Book I must surely be considered the lineal ancestor of this much-interrupted and frustrated serenade. Although the idea may be the same, the Cello Sonata is not merely a rehash of earlier work, but Debussy's complete re-imagining of the dramatic scenario, here with the added tonal resources of the cello and consequently a more evolved comic strategy.

The final movement (*Finale*), which follows the *Sérénade* without pause, is of another character altogether, although both instruments perform much guitar-like strumming and undergo many swift changes of mood. The movement opens in high spirits with a strumming for the pianist's left hand and a more urgent figuration in the right as the cello enters at 0:06 with the main theme, a long melody followed by a scampering figure (0:15). At 0:19 the instruments switch roles as the cellist, playing pizzicato, takes on the strumming while the pianist plays the scampering phrase. An abrupt slowdown at 0:26 changes the tone immediately from brisk to languid, with Moorish roulades for the piano as the cellist plucks notes (0:28–0:46).

The vigorous opening theme seems poised to return, but as he loved to do, Debussy frustrates his listeners with a series of different ideas, the first of which (0:55) is a brief passage played *"sur le chevalet"*—on the bridge of the cello, producing a bizarre, metallic sonority. Then the lead-in to the main theme appears again (1:00), but instead of the melody itself, what follows is an anxious passage in Debussy's trademark billowing harmony (1:03).

The music nearly stops at 1:17 as the cello plays a deeply lyrical episode, filled with drooping ornamental turns over gorgeous chords and arpeggios for the piano. This passage, in which Debussy asks the cellist to play "morbidly," is the movement's sorrowful center of gravity. But again the music begins to whirl at 2:10, leading at last into the reprise of the main theme group, first the soaring, long notes (2:30), followed by the scampering figure (2:38). The cello trills furiously as the piano takes over the racing figuration (2:42), then the anxious passage from earlier in the movement, now (2:46) hurried along at breakneck speed. At 2:50, the cello roars out a full-throated theme accompanied by furious boiling for the piano; three sudden, snapped chords for both instruments (2:55) bring back the guitar that was never far from Debussy's thoughts as he composed this characterful work. There is a final deceleration for the cello to sing out a grave phrase from the very beginning of the sonata (2:58), and the two instruments rush in to fling the Cello Sonata to a spirited, playful conclusion.

Everything about the Sonata for Flute, Viola, and Harp, also from 1915, is unusual. The uncommon instrumentation of three underlings, none capable of great power, immediately suggests that the music will be delicate or even ethereal. Indeed, neither blasting nor thumping are to be heard here, but Debussy manages to confound expectations with music that, while fine-boned, has a linear strength that is hard for the first-time listener to anticipate. Formally, its three movements are not in classical sonata form but are much closer to the sonata of the baroque era, in which each movement is based on a single motif, worked through in decorative fashion, although Debussy deploys more than one melody per section. He really uses the sonata title in its most basic sense, meaning an abstract sound piece. Above all, this sonata's flexibility of rhythm is the source of its hidden strength. Even as Debussy shifts between time signatures, the music moves with catlike, choreographic grace. This is also one of the composer's most wonderful experiments in pure sound, and it exudes the ecstasy of his final style, seeming at times to be lit from within.

The first movement, titled *Pastorale,* begins with a languid melody for the flute, significantly marked "melancholy," that seems to hover rather then move. But soon a more energetic episode in a swaying rhythm begins, with a danceable feel. The viola plays the brisk second subject in a skipping rhythm, which passes between the three instruments. The opening theme returns on the viola, followed again by the swaying episode; slowdowns in the tempo create a sense that the music is floating. The second movement, *Interlude,* is in the form of a minuet, the dignified dance of the eighteenth century. The flute states the melody, reminiscent of that of *Hommage à Rameau,* first, but all three instruments soon share it joyously. The momentum is carried gently to its end on a falling figure, stated by the flute—a dreamy, mystical theme full of inner fire, in which the viola joins, over sweeping arpeggios for the harp. The movement ends with a sad statement of the minuet melody.

The last movement (*Final,* in Debussy's term) opens with a bustling figure in the harp over which the viola and then the flute cry broken phrases, from which a long melody finally emerges. The viola picks up the rhythmic duty, but the atmosphere is heavy and anxious. Finally, the flute plays a determined theme, which soon fragments as the music broadens a bit. But before long the anxious tone returns, building to a stormy episode curiously reminiscent of *La mer.* Toward the end, a different, mystically joyous tone breaks through, and before the final chords sweep to the end, there is a recollection of the opening melody of the *Pastorale.*

The Sonata for Flute, Viola, and Harp is hardly Debussy's easiest piece, lacking as it does the kind of ordinary musical landmarks on which listeners depend. But it is great music, with its infinitely nuanced interweaving of melody, harmony, rhythm, and timbre demanding close attention. The surpassing strangeness of this singular work's instrumental sound, as well as its otherworldly blend of melancholy and spirituality, place the Sonata for Flute, Viola, and Harp in its own class, even in a canon of work as mold-breaking as Debussy's.

Debussy composed the Sonata for Violin and Piano with considerable struggle in 1916 and 1917. It is his last work, as well as the last he played in public, at its premiere in May 1917. Cancer had finally overtaken the composer, draining him and finally demolishing the eruption of creativity that began in 1915. Almost from the start, critics have found the Violin Sonata to be on a lower level than its companions, Lockspeiser, for instance, calling it "an illuminating failure" (164). Critics' discontents focus on the sonata's musical content, which is perhaps less imaginative than that of its bold companion works, and its form, which is a blend of traditional classical sonata with the cyclical form Debussy had employed in the String Quartet. It is peculiar and perhaps a little sad that Debussy found the need to fall back on the form he had made pointless over the course of his career, but the Violin Sonata offers much to admire nonetheless.

The Violin Sonata's first movement opens with a long and beautiful theme built of a falling pattern followed by a swirling melodic turn; the second theme is a fervent, narrow melody played on the fingerboard, giving it a breathless intensity. The development section plays this and the opening melody off each other in a fairly traditional manner, over a gorgeously dreamy arpeggio piano accompaniment. The opening melody returns quietly, and the movement ends in a forceful passage that is both waltz-like and Spanish flavored.

The second movement is another fantastical serenade, rather like that of the Cello Sonata, but without the malicious humor that makes that great movement fly. The finale opens with a statement of the first melody of the opening movement over spectral rumbling for the piano. The scampering main theme is interrupted several times by slower sections replete with mock-passionate gestures, and the coda is built of a falling figure close in profile to the first-movement theme. There are two witty false endings, after which the music seems to wind itself up again in a final, surprisingly high-spirited scramble to the finish.

With its many beautiful themes, this piece appeals easily to audiences. But like most of Debussy's music—like most *music,* for that matter—the Violin Sonata depends on performers who believe in what they are playing. The famous 1940 Library of Congress performance of the Violin Sonata by the great Hungarian violinist Joseph Szigeti accompanied by composer Béla Bartók—the marvelous disciple of Debussy's music—is one of the greatest recorded examples of skilled performers carrying out this lovely, flawed reflection of Debussy's declining health with their virtuosity and passionate conviction.

The Quiet Revolutionary

ebussy's significance in the history of music is difficult to overestimate: he turned the art on its head in the tumultuous quarter-century of his creative maturity, from 1893 to 1918. So enormous were his innovations that no serious, progressive composer who followed has been able to ignore Debussy's liberation of harmony from outworn rules and his forging of forms that grow out of the musical material, rather than fitting ideas into preconceived forms. The difficulty of coming up with a steady stream of self-sufficient ideas of a quality and density comparable to Debussy's sent some running to the safe harbor of a "new" formalism.

But above all, Debussy's insistence on sound itself as the dominant element in his music set the course for the near-century of music that has followed. The bravest musical experiments of the twentieth century by Stravinsky, Bartók, Varèse, Carter, Boulez, Nono, Stockhausen, Messiaen, and Xenakis are inconceivable without Debussy's quiet revolution. From the dizzy complexities of *Jeux* to the single line of flute melody that is *Syrinx,* Debussy conceived his music in terms of pure timbre, and this joy in shimmering sound, imagined for its own sensuous beauty, overwhelmed his followers.

Debussy's music is tough-minded, sophisticated stuff that challenges the intellect and emotions, not to mention the listener's expectations of how music behaves. There are great composers—Handel, Beethoven, Chopin, and Verdi, for example—whose music speaks with reasonable directness. Debussy's, quite deliberately, does not, so that a surprising number of professional musicians and serious listeners are incapable of enjoying it. Some grudgingly appreciate Debussy's harmonic courage and his reconception of instrumental tone color as a primary compositional element. But they miss from his melodies the kind of strong profiles they are used to and, above all, cannot fathom his rejection of traditional developmental processes. In other words, they don't like his tunes or the way he works them through. Yet as shown by the *Prélude à l'après-midi d'un faune,* the long excerpt from *Pelléas et Mélisande,* and the piano prelude *La fille aux cheveux de lin,* all on the CD at the back of this book, long, lush melodies came as easily to Debussy as they did to Puccini. And *La mer* and *Ibéria* prove that he could build big climaxes that equal those by the greatest symphonic masters. How, then, to begin to break through the multiple difficulties of this thorny, allusive music?

The keys for the troubled listener are to accept that Debussy's innovations are deliberate as well as immense and to let go of expectations based on the work of almost any composer who preceded him. Debussy's music follows different logical and emotional trajectories, consistently frustrating listeners who insist on looking for conventional patterns. One must accept that Debussy's music moves in unexpected ways and must listen to where it travels, instead of waiting in anxious irritation for what it does not do. Gradually but surely, its power, beauty, and sense become overwhelmingly apparent. After one acclimates to his musical language, Debussy opens one's ears once and for all, sometimes making the ordinary patterns of fugue, sonata, and rondo sound predictable and trite. One comes to crave the potent magnetic pull of his inner direction and follows gratefully where he courageously leads.

Debussy's music is paradoxically highly evolved and subrational, speaking with clarity of a deeper, dreamlike level of consciousness. Below the mysterious beauty of Debussy's musical surfaces lurk crosscurrents seductive and dangerous, and bottomless depths.

Selected Bibliography

Cobb, Margaret G., annotator. *Debussy's Letters to Ingelbrecht: The Story of a Musical Friendship*. Rochester, New York: University of Rochester Press, 2005.

Kerman, Joseph. *Opera as Drama*. New York: Vintage Books, 1956.

Lesure, François, collector and with introduction by, and Richard Langham Smith, translator and editor. *Debussy on Music: The Critical Writings of the Great French Composer Claude Debussy*. Ithaca, New York: Cornell University Press, 1988.

Lockspeiser, Edward. *Debussy*. London: J. M. Dent and Sons, 1936. Revised edition, 1951.

Nichols, Roger. *Debussy Remembered*. London: Faber and Faber, 1992. North American edition: Portland, Oregon: Amadeus Press, 1992.

Nichols, Roger. *The Life of Debussy*. Cambridge, England: Cambridge University Press, 1998.

Nichols, Roger, and Richard Langham Smith, editors. *Claude Debussy: Pelléas et Mélisande*. Cambridge, England: Cambridge University Press, 1989.

Roberts, Paul. *Images: The Piano Music of Claude Debussy*. Portland, Oregon: Amadeus Press, 1996.

Samson, Jim, editor. *The Cambridge Companion to Chopin*. Cambridge, England: Cambridge University Press, 1992.

Schmitz, E. Robert. *The Piano Works of Claude Debussy*. Mineola, New York: Dover, 1966.

Stravinsky, Igor. *An Autobiography*. New York: W. W. Norton, 1962.

Weaver, William, and Martin Chusid, editors. *The Verdi Companion*. New York: W. W. Norton, 1979.

8. *Les collines d'Anacapri* (no. 5 of *Préludes I*) (3:18)
    Arturo Benedetti Michelangeli, piano.
    CD 469 827-2.

9. *La fille aux cheveux de lin* (no. 8 of *Préludes I*) (2:54)
    Arturo Benedetti Michelangeli, piano.
    CD 469 827-2.

10. *Brouillards* (no. 1 of *Préludes II*) (3:58)
    Arturo Benedetti Michelangeli, piano.
    CD 469 828-2.

11. *La terrasse des audiences du clair de lune* (no. 7 of *Préludes II*) (3:58)
    Arturo Benedetti Michelangeli, piano.
    CD 469 828-2.

12. *Feux d'artifice* (no. 12 of *Préludes II*) (4:34)
    Arturo Benedetti Michelangeli, piano.
    CD 469 828-2.

13. *Beau soir* (2:29)
    Gerard Souzay, baritone, and Dalton Baldwin, piano.
    CD 463 664-2.

14. Cello Sonata in D minor: *Prologue*: Lent (4:54)
    Mischa Maisky, cello, and Martha Argerich, piano.
    CD 289 471 3462.

15. Cello Sonata in D minor: *Sérénade*: Modérément animé (3:37)
    Mischa Maisky, cello, and Martha Argerich, piano.
    CD 289 471 3462.

16. Cello Sonata in D minor: *Finale*: Animé (3:44)
    Mischa Maisky, cello, and Martha Argerich, piano.
    CD 289 471 3462.

CD Track Listing

1. *Prélude à l'après-midi d'un faune* (8:54)
   The Cleveland Orchestra, Pierre Boulez conducting.
   CD 435 766-2.

2. *Pelléas et Mélisande,* act 3, scene 1: "Mes longs cheveux descendent jusqu'au seuil de la tour" (5:59)
   Maria Ewing (Mélisande), François Le Roux (Pelléas), José van Dam (Golaud); Vienna Philharmonic, Claudio Abbado conducting.
   CD 435 344-2.

3. *Pelléas et Mélisande,* act 3, scene 1: "Je les tiens dans les mains" (4:11)
   Maria Ewing (Mélisande), François Le Roux (Pelléas), José van Dam (Golaud); Vienna Philharmonic, Claudio Abbado conducting.
   CD 435 344-2.

4. *Pelléas et Mélisande,* act 3, scene 1: "Que faites vous ici?" (3:32)
   Maria Ewing (Mélisande), François Le Roux (Pelléas), José van Dam (Golaud); Vienna Philharmonic, Claudio Abbado conducting.
   CD 435 344-2.

5. *Soirée dans Grenade* (no. 2 of *Estampes*) (5:14)
   Sviatoslav Richter, piano.
   CD 457 667-2.

6. *Reflets dans l'eau* (no. 1 of *Images I*) (4:53)
   Arturo Benedetti Michelangeli, piano.
   CD 469 828-2.

7. *Hommage à Rameau* (no. 2 of *Images I*) (6:34)
   Arturo Benedetti Michelangeli, piano.
   CD 469 828-2.